"Beth and Sarah wrote the book we want and need for right now. In this story-driven guide, they provide a road map to having hard conversations and tackling tough topics with grace and care. Their suggestions and examples will bolster your confidence to discuss fraught issues in a way that bridges the gap between you and your loved ones instead of shutting down communication. (If you were to jot down their conversational prompts on index cards to keep in your pocket for easy reference before your next family gathering, I wouldn't blame you a bit!) Even in these difficult times, this dependable author duo makes readers feel like we really might be able to all move forward, together."

Anne Bogel, host of *What Should I Read Next* podcast

"Lively and accessible and smart, *Now What?* addresses the human condition and the complications that have made so many Americans feel divided and disheartened in their politics and their personal lives. With a fresh approach and some good faith, the cohosts of the podcast *Pantsuit Politics* argue, conflict can be used to strengthen connections, not sever them."

Susan Page, Washington bureau chief of *USA Today* and *New York Times* bestselling author of *Madam Speaker*

"This book is a bighearted, clear-eyed look at the polarized world we find ourselves in—with real guidance on how to move forward."

Anne Helen Peterson, author of *Can't Even*

"In *Now What?* Sarah and Beth challenge us to see the connections we share as human beings—from our closest friends to the fellow citizens we may never meet. Then, just as they have done for years on their podcast, they empower us through curiosity and grace to strengthen these connections that hold us up and hold us together. We need this book now more than ever."

Gretchen Carlson, acclaimed journalist, female empowerment advocate, and cofounder of Lift Our Voices

"It is no secret that Beth and Sarah have long been my North Star for a nuanced approach to political discussion without all the bias. What a thrill to read their latest work—that our shared conflicts can actually create deeper connections with people? I'll have what they are having. Beth and Sarah are the living best at reclaiming common ground."

Jen Hatmaker, speaker, podcast host, and *New York Times* bestselling author of *Fierce, Free, and Full of Fire*

"Sarah and Beth have somehow figured out a way to approach every discussion with grace, composure, and wisdom, and listening to them will make you a better person."

Clint Harp, TV/podcast host and author of *Handcrafted*

"Sarah and Beth are two of my favorite grown-ups because they are honest about both the best and the worst of us. They never allow us to draw sweeping conclusions about anything, especially each other. If we're going to learn how to move forward together, then we need trustworthy guides for the journey. This is the book to help us make amends, increase the good, and learn how to show up for each other even when we disagree."

Emily P. Freeman, *Wall Street Journal* bestselling author of *The Next Right Thing*

"This isn't a book about politics; it's a book about empathy. At a time when we just want to be better humans, Beth and Sarah show us the way."

Kendra Adachi, *New York Times* bestselling author of *The Lazy Genius Way*

"Reflective, smart, a breath of fresh air that captures our humanity during a time of division and uncertainty. Overcoming polarization in our country begins with grace by reading *Now What?* and by listening to Sarah and Beth. A must-read for anyone who wishes to build connection, search for solutions, and promote healing for family, community, and nation."

Amy McGrath, retired Marine Corps fighter pilot, former candidate for US Senate, and author of *Honor Bound*

"As the world begins to reemerge from the chaos of the last few years, we look to our friends Sarah and Beth to help us make sense of 'what now?' In their comforting but honest way, these creators of community invite us to remain active in the work of our lives: committing to the hard and holy process of loving other people, even when what they believe is an affront to what we hold dear. There's no better guide for how to actually connect, how to manage our own expectations, and how to genuinely love (not just tolerate) those we vehemently disagree with. I'm so grateful we live in a world with Sarahs and Beths."

Erin Moon, resident Bible scholar on *The Bible Binge* podcast and author of *O Heavy Lightness, Every Broken Thing*, and *Memento Mori*

"There is no magic elixir, as Sarah and Beth would say, to solve division in our world. But there is a magic mindset, and these two women have it. With personal stories and practical advice, they show us how to love our neighbors—which includes our families—and make peace with discomfort. If you, like me, would occasionally prefer locking your door and holing up with a tub of cookie dough instead of dealing with other humans, you need this book."

Elizabeth Passarella, author of *Good Apple*

"*Now What?* is an essential read for our toxic time. In an era of profound division and pain, Sarah and Beth help us see the power we have to heal the world. It rests in the relationships we already have—at home and across the globe. Read this book and discover a path forward paved with curiosity, grace, and connection."

Lisa Sharon Harper, president and founder of Freedom Road and author of *The Very Good Gospel* and *Fortune*

"I look to Sarah and Beth for rational takes on the irrational state of politics. Their podcasts and first book helped me so much when I was changing political parties many years ago, and *Now What?* is the next stage of the conversation for those of us who have been floundering politically. Read this book if you're looking for political calm in all the noise."

Laura Tremaine, author of *Share Your Stuff. I'll Go First.*

"Perhaps you found yourself sitting in the break room or in the church pew or at your own Thanksgiving table when you heard an opinion that startled you into disbelief. Maybe that disbelief quickly worked its way through your system until you were screaming at your boss, your small group leader, or your aunt Gladys. How do we remain connected to those we like and love who see the world so differently from us? In *Now What?*, Sarah and Beth are our captains, helping us chart a course in the rocky waters of relationships and politics. This book is a compass pointing us to where the calm seas meet our inclination to curse out Aunt Gladys."

Jamie B. Golden, cohost of *The Popcast* and *The Bible Binge* podcasts

NOW
What?

HOW TO MOVE FORWARD
WHEN WE'RE DIVIDED
(ABOUT BASICALLY EVERYTHING)

SARAH STEWART HOLLAND
AND BETH SILVERS

Revell

a division of Baker Publishing Group
Grand Rapids, Michigan

Published by Revell
a division of Baker Publishing Group
PO Box 6287, Grand Rapids, MI 49516-6287
www.revellbooks.com

Printed in the United States of America

Library of Congress Cataloging-in-Publication Data
Names: Stewart Holland, Sarah, author. | Silvers, Beth, 1981– author.
Title: Now what? / Sarah Stewart Holland and Beth Silvers.
Description: Grand Rapids, MI : Revell, a division of Baker Publishing Group, 2022. | Includes bibliographical references.
Identifiers: LCCN 2021041424 | ISBN 9780800740801 | ISBN 9781493436415 (ebook)
Subjects: LCSH: Interpersonal conflict—United States. | Conflict management—United States. | Polarization (Social sciences)—United States. | Interpersonal relations—United States.
Classification: LCC HM132 .S7273 2022 | DDC 306.20973—dc23
LC record available at https://lccn.loc.gov/2021041424

Baker Publishing Group publications use paper produced from sustainable forestry practices and post-consumer waste whenever possible.

22 23 24 25 26 27 28   7 6 5 4 3 2 1

To Nicholas and Chad,
who keep us moving forward
with their love and support.

CONTENTS

Introduction   13

PART ONE   THOSE CLOSEST TO US   20

1. Our Families of Origin: Don't Question
   Grandma and Other Unwritten Rules   23

2. The Families We Create: We Are More Than
   Our Opinions about Julia Roberts   47

3. Raising Citizens: "Everything's Going to Be All
   Right" and Other Lies We Tell Kids   67

4. Friendships: Best Friends Forever . . . or Until
   We Disagree   85

5. Workplaces: From the Food Chain
   to the Garden   103

PART TWO   THOSE FARTHER AWAY   120

6. Community—Churches and Nonprofits
   and Schools: Why Churches Don't Belong
   on Yelp   123

7. Local and State Government: Culture Wars and Poop   151

8. National Politics: You Deal with Your Pain Your Way, I Deal with My Pain Mine   167

9. Social Media: Twitter Ain't Church, but a Group Might Be Good for Your Soul   183

10. Global Politics: Future Problem-Solving Forever   201

Conclusion   217

Appendix: When Connections Are Too Toxic and Need to Be Severed   223

Acknowledgments   227

Notes   229

We are like islands in the sea,
separate on the surface
but connected in the deep.

WILLIAM JAMES

INTRODUCTION

"Now what?"

It's the question we encounter more than any other.

The election is over. Now what?

We survived a disaster. Now what?

We had a terrible argument about politics and everything's awkward. Now what?

I tried to disagree graciously. Now what?

We talked it over but it still feels like we live on different planets. Now what?

We all agree we have big problems to solve. Now what?

We started a podcast to talk about politics as citizens, not as pundits, journalists, or politicians. We wanted to hold ourselves accountable to a different way of communicating and, in the process, perhaps set an example that might be helpful to others. We've been at the work of grace-filled discussions since 2015. We've made hundreds of hours of podcasts, written a book, and traveled the country talking with audiences in person about moving toward healthier relationships around politics. While it has been the most rewarding work of our lives, we won't lie to you, it can be hard to feel that we're making even the tiniest of dents in a political landscape that's driven by conflict.

In our first book, *I Think You're Wrong (But I'm Listening): A Guide to Grace-Filled Political Conversations*, we argued that we should all take off our partisan team jerseys.

We wrote:

> For most people who are passionate about politics . . . , there are two teams: Democrats vs. Republicans, conservatives vs. liberals, right vs. left. Many of us are born into one of the two and are taught by our parents and community that only one party could possibly represent our values . . . we put on our team jerseys and adopt the policies, positions, and politicians expected of us.[1]

Several years later, we've realized that describing party identification as a jersey was a very optimistic metaphor. Party identity has become so strong it can become even more important than identities used to define us as human beings: father, sister, friend, American, church member, Christian. And some of us are now willing to sacrifice those other identities (and the relationships that go with them) on the altar of our political identity. Today, partisan jerseys feel less like clothing we can easily shed and more like a tattoo—it can come off, but the removal is a tough process.

We could write fifty books analyzing how we got here and why this polarization is harmful, but we don't think that's helpful (plus, there are already *loads* of books on that topic). Paraphrasing author and speaker Byron Katie in *Loving What Is: Four Questions That Can Change Your Life*, we're welcome to fight with reality, but reality will always win. Accepting that some people are deeply wedded to their partisan labels, we also have to acknowledge that there are big questions our political parties will not be able to answer for us. And, as critical as politics is to how we live in community together, it cannot be the only container for working out our identities and values.

Plus, one of the cruelest aspects of this pervasive sense of constant conflict is the shrinking of our timelines. Anxiety and fear tell us that things are the worst they've ever been and cannot get better unless we go to war with each other. But the truth is, going to war with one another is a zero-sum idea. In war, either as a nation or between friends, someone has to win and someone has to lose. More conflict is not the answer. *We don't think most of us are looking for victory. We're looking for connection.*

As we spend time with people across the United States, conversations that often begin about seemingly intractable political conflict lead to deeper questions about separation. "How do I know when my dad has become so toxic that I need to cut him out of my life?" "Does this mean it's time for me to get a divorce?" "Maybe I can't be friends with her anymore." "They don't seem to accept me, so maybe I should just leave." From our listeners and readers, we see, hear, and feel a pervasive sense of loneliness.

And it's not just within our community. From the nightly news to our social media feeds, a drumbeat of messages tells us that we can't do it. We are polarized, divided, *strangers to one another*. Those messages are disseminated through the lens of politics, but they resonate more generally. It's no wonder that loneliness and depression are rampant for individuals and that populism and nationalism are rampant for countries.

We are facing a new experiment in human history, and what we face is less a political question than a civic one: How do we live in diverse societies when the historical crutches of religion, ethnicity, or even geography are no longer as powerful as they once were? How do we find connection to one another when our differences are constantly on display? How can we strengthen our connections to one another when politics threatens to tear us apart?

In other words, now what?

It's become so clear to us that most political conflict is wrapped around deeper emotional and spiritual dynamics— dynamics that might be painful to examine but that have the capacity to help us grow and heal far beyond partisan battles. In this book, we attempt to zoom out and see what larger issues are at the center of our political conflicts, whether they take place inside our families, our workplaces, our communities, our country, or our world. We've been intentionally practicing that mining process: What's underneath this conversation? How do we bring it into the light? How do we find something good in that light? We want to share what we've learned here, in the hopes that you'll find new questions or phrases to help you dig deeper in your relationships.

To do that, we believe we have to reexamine all the levels of connection in our lives: from our families of origin to the entire human race with which we share this planet. We aren't going to be able to give you hard-and-fast rules at any of these levels. (We know everyone wants a quick and easy rule about ghosting your uncle on Facebook. It doesn't exist. We're sorry!)

Here's what we hope to do throughout this book:

- help us all see these levels of connection more clearly and the factors beyond politics that might be at play in those relationships
- share stories that help us know we aren't alone and from which we might be able to gain some inspiration
- draw on historic examples of connection to reorient us as family members, friends, colleagues, neighbors, and global citizens
- look to the future with our problem-solving hats on so that we can confidently and compassionately navigate our personal and civic challenges

We know and experience the deep worry associated with pervasive polarization. This book is not intended to add to your worries. We want to relieve some pressure by saying as clearly as we can, "We have urgent problems, and you don't have to solve them all because you are not alone."

This book is also not intended to guilt you into staying in toxic spaces. There are times when some level of separation is the right answer—whether that means separating from a person, a job, or an institution. We're here to help you ask questions about when to separate and when to stay. We're here to help you think about the impact of your connections.

We don't want to focus only on your painful relationships. If we've learned anything since the beginning of our partnership, it's that building on the strength of healthy relationships creates so many possibilities and sustains us through tough times. We also write this book with an enduring and deep humility. We are experts only in our own experiences, and our experiences don't represent everyone.

We are as we seem on the surface: two middle-class white ladies—both former lawyers, both living in Kentucky, both happily married to men, both raising little kids. Despite these similarities, when we started our podcast in 2015, we felt like strangers to one another. We knew the loose outlines of one another's lives from our time together in college, and we knew we were (at the time) on different sides of the political spectrum. Our differences were on full display during a time in American history when differences were all that mattered. And yet—over the past seven years—we have built a successful partnership and life-giving friendship together, not by avoiding our differences or conflicts (political or otherwise) but by connecting through them. That connection has allowed us to see both our politics and ourselves more clearly. It has allowed us to dig deep beneath the anger and the fear to the problems we face in our communities, in our nation, and in our world with a more complex and complete perspective. It has allowed us to work toward a solution together, instead of trying to fix the problem on our own.

That's what we're inviting you to do in these pages. We're inviting you to see the connections you hold with fellow human beings in a bigger way—from the people in your home you see every day to the people across the globe you never meet.

We will begin with our closest connections—our family, our friends, our coworkers—and look at what political conflict can teach us about ourselves and others. Then, with fresh eyes, we hope to expand into the other connections we hold with our fellow human beings—in our communities, states, nation, and world—to see beyond the political morass to how we can continue on . . . *together*.

Now what?

We all want the answers to be: Now, we solve the problem. Now, we all agree. Now, we all stop fighting. But we all know deep down that is never going to happen. Instead, we're inviting you to see *Now What?* not as an opportunity to *solve* conflict but to *use* it to connect more deeply with the people around you.

Part One

THOSE CLOSEST TO US

The best way to examine our connections (and what's keeping us divided) is to start with those closest to us. In the first half of the book, we're going to look at our most intimate connections and what political conflict can teach us about what's buried deep beneath fights over Facebook and battles across the dinner table. We start with our families of origin and what generational expectations can help parents and children and siblings and even extended family understand about one another. We then look at our families of choice—our romantic mates, our parenting partners, those we have brought close to us by design—and think about what (and who) we're trying to control when we fight about our ballots or our candidates. Next, we take a moment to examine how caregivers talk to the children in their lives about politics. (Spoiler: you already have everything you need for these conversations!) Finally, we look at the other people in our day-to-day lives: our friends and our coworkers. Our closest friendships are so frequently built on similarity; our political views usually expose our differences. As we're learning to show up as our whole selves with family and friends, we examine how we can face our fears and do the same at work.

1

Our Families of Origin

Don't Question Grandma and Other Unwritten Rules

Sarah: In the fall of 2019, Beth and I traveled to California for two live shows—one in San Francisco and one in Los Angeles. My dad has lived in California since I was five years old, and I spent most every summer of my childhood visiting him in the Golden State. However, Beth had never been out west, and I thought taking the Pacific Coast Highway between our two shows would make the most of our short trip. My dad is incredibly generous and loves to drive, so he volunteered to make the trip up and back from Bakersfield where he lives in one day. The three of us spent almost twelve hours together in the car, taking in the gorgeous coastline and eating lots of In-N-Out. My dad and I both love music, so we also spent a lot of time sharing new bands we'd found and singing along to nineties country where our tastes consistently converge.

It sounds lovely, doesn't it? A devoted father bonding with his daughter, surrounded by a panorama of blue skies and crashing waves with Garth Brooks serenading us in the background. (FYI our DMs are closed to alternate opinions of Garth Brooks.) Of course, the reality is more complicated. At that point in 2019, we were over two years into the Trump presidency. There had been two years of tweets and chaos. There had been two years of anger and fear and frustration . . . for me. My dad voted for Trump proudly, and his continued support for the president had become a constant source of conflict within our relationship. For the majority of our trip we steered clear of politics as most American families were at least attempting to do at that point (if they were still talking at all). But Beth's presence—and her recent change in party registration from Republican to Democrat—was something my dad couldn't ignore. He knew where I stood, after all, but he seemed sincerely curious about where Beth was (and how she got there), so on occasion, a rather intense exchange on politics would surface as we made our way down the coast. It was like an episode of *The View* crossed with a car commercial.

I remember we talked about Hillary Clinton (of course) and immigration and race. It was like the greatest hits of polarized politics with the greatest hits of Reba, Shania, and Trisha playing in the background. We didn't solve anything on that trip. My dad ended the day just as devoted to Trump as when we began, and I ended it just as disgusted with Trump as when we began. It was fun and it was also stressful, which can describe almost every single family gathering, in my opinion. However, it was Beth's observation afterward that helped me see my dad—and our relationship—with new eyes.

She said after watching us in the car for all those hours, she realized that my dad and I had different expectations when it came to conflict. I expected the presence of conflict and was fine holding the tension of that disagreement. I knew she was right. I don't expect us to come to a compromise and agreement when we talk politics. I would be lying if I said I don't want to influence my dad, but I have no expectation of fundamentally changing him or his opinions when it comes to Trump or anything else political. However, she also said that my dad did not expect the presence of conflict and therefore the tension of the disagreement was really hard on him. Not until she pointed that out did I realize how right she was. My dad seems genuinely confused and hurt when I see things differently than him. He uses the word *disrespect* a lot. He often thinks I'm angry with him when I am not. It is as if he expects a healthy relationship to not have any conflict. Unfortunately that's not how I operate. Since that trip, I've tried to remember that our political disagreement doesn't exist in a vacuum. Like Reba and Garth on the best road trip, our different expectations of each other are always playing in the background.

....

Before we belong to ourselves, we belong to the people who raise us.

Before we can form the conscious thoughts that are the building blocks of our identity, we belong to our parents and to our families of origin. Belonging to our families of origin is that first connection. It is the sense that we belong as members of this—our first and most important—group. Belonging is essential because we are dependent on our families for our very survival. As babies that belonging is as basic as food and shelter. But if we learn the importance of belonging through our dependence on our families as vulnerable infants, we soon realize that belonging to our families also meets deeper and more complicated emotional needs. Belonging helps us find value in life, cope with painful experiences, improve our motivation, and know that we aren't alone. It all starts with our families.

From the people who raise us, we learn what to value, how to be in relationships, and what patterns of behavior help us thrive. The warmth, security, and boundaries of our caregivers shape our development in conscious and unconscious ways for the rest of our lives.[1] If we have siblings, they shape our understanding of our own strengths, our conflict styles, and our resilience.[2]

Our families of origin make us who we are, and that's why a breakdown in those connections hurts so badly.

Although it always feels unique, personal, and urgent, political conflict within families is not new. These conflicts have long been fertile ground for storytellers and screenwriters. Political divisions have been depicted in Shakespearean drama, in the Bunkers' battling over civil rights on *All in the Family*, and in Alex P. Keaton's decision to join the Reagan Revolution on *Family Ties*. Today, shows like *Blackish* tackle complex and conflicting generational attitudes toward colorism and other issues of identity.

And yet, as much as America loves stories about familial conflict, we don't do a very good job showing how to work through those conflicts. There's no laugh track in real life to get us through awkward moments at the dinner table when our great-aunt says something racist. There are no closing credits to cue us into a neat and tidy resolution to the latest fight over a viral YouTube video.

We need something in the era of the Politicization of Everything, because our families of origin are suffering under the increased weight of partisanship and identity politics. These disagreements have very real consequences. Identity politics are not theoretical, and our politics increasingly say something meaningful about how we value each other. When politics represents who we are, what does it mean when our family disagrees with us?

These are the most heartbreaking stories we hear from our community: fathers who seem like strangers to their daughters, sons who slowly shut their parents out of their lives, mothers who wield shame as a weapon to assure party loyalty, siblings who no longer speak, people who are not accepted as who they are by the people who gave them life. When these divisions infect our families, it can create a crisis around our sense of belonging. It can feel like a problem that we must solve, and in the process, we can create and endure an enormous amount of suffering.

We receive more emails every week about navigating political conflict within families than any other topic. People want us to tell them how to fix it, and we dearly wish we could. We wish we had a formula, an elixir, some way to prescribe adjustments to an attitude here and to media consumption there so that the wheels of communication start turning again. People aren't machines, and the tension among us isn't a math problem. Instead of trying to fix the partisan divides in our families, we are working to try to *see* them better. We're trying to lift ourselves out of the present—where we're mired in sadness and anger and disbelief—so that we can better understand the dynamics. What's really going on?

Different Experiences Mean Different Expectations

A decent percentage of our email might as well have the subject line: "[Insert politician or pundit name] is wrecking my family." Whether it's about who we've voted for, which cable news channel we default to, or what podcast host gets our listening time, individuals representing partisan positions tend to capture our imaginations and, with them, our identities. In our families, this identification leads to conversations and text threads that look like:

HOW COULD YOU POSSIBLY LISTEN
TO THIS GARBAGE?

> HOW COULD YOU NOT?
> YOU'RE MISSING EVERYTHING.

All-caps conversations are rarely helpful, but as we're going to learn over and over in the pages of this book, we're actually having two conversations at once. We're not just talking about commentators or channels; we're talking about our relationship with each other and how we're showing up in it. We are working out our conflict styles as much as we are working out our political differences.

Some of the disconnection within our families of origin that *feels* like political disagreement can best be understood as generational conflict. Sometimes when we're raging over a certain politician or commentator, we're actually fighting about different expectations.

Lindsay Pollak, an expert on the multigenerational workplace, has spent years examining generations and how they interact—not just in the US but around the globe. "I don't think there's any fundamental way that we are different as human beings for being in different generations," she says. "It just changes your expectations."[3] Unfortunately, the prolific media coverage of cross-generational conflict often leaves the expectations of each group unexamined. It's never that one generation has different understandings and expectations surrounding race or gender or work but rather that one generation has an opinion that the other generation sees as wrong. (Not to mention, not everyone in a generation feels the exact same way about everything. We were born the same year as Beyoncé but—as much as we secretly believe we share a lot in common with Queen Bey—we recognize the babies of 1981 are not a monolith any more than the babies of 1964.)

> **Sometimes when we're raging over a certain politician or commentator, we're actually fighting about different expectations.**

Fostering generational conflict might make for some good memes and *Saturday Night Live* sketches, but oversimplifying that conflict is not serving us. We're missing out on important information about each other. "OK Boomer" or eye-rolling about Gen Z deprives us of critical context about each other's histories, cohorts, and personal stories.

The beauty of each individual human experience is both its uniqueness and its mystery. We will never understand what it was like to birth us, feed us, change our diapers, and send us to time-out. This leaves a certain formative amount of loved ones perspectives unknowable to us. It also leaves us blind to what we can know about the experiences of our caregivers and siblings. How often do we think about how our mother's military service might give her a different perspective on authority than we have? When do we stop to consider whether a brother's concern about our job change reflects the insecurity associated with a traumatic childhood experience? It's easy to forget that our grandparents' experiences in the 1960s inform their perspectives on movements like Occupy Wall Street and Defund the Police.

Instead of naming what we know and don't know about each other, many of us tend to operate from the unarticulated expectation that every person in our family shared the same experiences we had and processed those experiences the same way. When we operate from that assumption, it's disorienting that a sibling prefers Fox News to our MSNBC or that our aunt who raised us voted for the Senate candidate we can't stand. The more we can name what we know about all the factors that shape us as people, the more light we can shine on the origins of our political differences.

And here's a bonus: the act of telling stories is one of the most connecting experiences we can have. Most of us are bursting with stories we'd love for someone to listen to (perhaps for the fifteenth time). Even painful, largely untold stories can forge beautiful bonds.

These differences extend far beyond our individual experiences. If you feel like your Baby Boomer father or your Generation Z daughter lives in a different reality, you're not wrong! Our grandmothers grew up without television and with the profound fallout of World War II and the Great Depression (hence Beth's grandmother recycling pieces of aluminum foil). Our parents grew up without the internet and came of age during the traumatic upheaval of the 1960s. Our children will ride in self-driving cars, will view 9/11 as a distant historic event, and will have few, if any, memories of the Trump administration or the COVID-19 pandemic.

Making the Connection

If you're struggling in a relationship with a family member, spend a moment making a list of things you know about that person. When you look at that list, do you see points that might create a deeper connection between you? Do you see points that might be the source of your differing perspectives?

What happens when you do this same exercise while considering a family member you feel genuinely close to?

We Expect to Argue Differently (or Not Argue at All)

The timing of our births influences so many of our expectations about the world. It also influences our expectations surrounding conflict itself—where should conflict be present? How should we deal with it? What does conflict mean inside a close family relationship?

Beth: When I was eleven (eleven and three-fourths, I would have insisted), my parents had a second child. My beloved sister, Kimberly, went to kindergarten the year I went to college. On September 11, 2001, I was a junior in college who watched the second plane crash into the World Trade Center and called my dad to ask him what it meant for the world. Kimberly was not yet nine years old. I logged in to my first email account as a senior in high school. Kimberly had an online profile from elementary school.

The external world isn't the only sphere of profound difference for the two of us. Our mom threw softballs and jumped on the trampoline with me. When Kimberly was young, Mom was in the early stages of a severe rheumatoid arthritis diagnosis. Our grandmother, Joy, was my best friend and constant companion growing up. Kimberly would say the same of her. But we experienced very different versions of Grandmother Joy because of the impacts of dementia. Kimberly grew up with cousins that I barely know. I remember relatives she never met.

I think I saw Kimberly as my baby sister until she was well into adulthood. After all, I loaded her up in my Mercury Topaz and took her to preschool every day. I was in a car accident my junior year of high school that was in some ways a defining event in my life. Five-year-old Kimberly was in the back seat. We experienced that event, literally and figuratively, from very different seats.

When I went to college, Kimberly visited me with dolls in tow. When she went to college, she brought her laundry to my house and babysat my daughters. It wasn't until she married, moved to Chicago, renovated a house, and had her own child, that I started seeing her as a peer.

Kimberly and I didn't learn to fight with each other. Because of our age difference, my sister and I didn't have that childhood laboratory of working out disagreements over toys and activities and who hogs the bathroom mirror. I wouldn't change a single dimension of our relationship. (Well, I do wish she would move into my neighborhood, but other than that . . .) And yet, as I watch my daughters, who are only four years apart, duke it out every day over the swings and shoes and who touched this coloring book, I find myself wondering what Kimberly and I missed about how to vigorously argue with people and love them anyway.

Sometimes I wonder how our lack of practice with conflict will play out as we grow older and life gets harder. We love each other fiercely. Do we know how to argue with each other if we truly disagree when difficult decisions about our parents' health or property have to be made? I know we can work through these things. Also I'm already thinking about how to show Kimberly that I'm her peer. When it's time to make those critical, complex choices, I don't want to be in the "big sister" role. I want us to be two equals, working together to figure out the best path forward for our family.

....

Some of us grow up in households where sharp words are never uttered. Some of us grow up in households where language and dishes fly. In some households, an argument means prolonged periods of silence and the withholding of affection. In others, raised voices are quickly followed by laughter. In some families, it's seen as completely disrespectful to question an elder. In others, it's seen as intellectually lazy to accept all family orthodoxy.

33

The unwritten rules around who we argue with and how we have those arguments are the results of generations of patterns. These patterns create a set of expectations that we too frequently forget to discuss. It's helpful to remember when political topics come up that we are talking about and working on so much more than policy, electoral, or even cultural disagreement. We might be talking *about* Obamacare, but we are talking *around* our different understandings of the world and different expectations about conflict.

Making the Connection

We want to stop talking around those different expectations and start getting to the heart of our disagreements. One way to do that is through storytelling. When we ask each other open-ended and unexpected questions, we can learn more about what's behind the opinions and emotions that can make some of our closest relationships so difficult.

As a few examples:

- If you're talking to a family member about immigration and are surprised at the distance between your stances, you might say, "Isn't it interesting that we grew up in the same place, went to church together, know lots of the same people, and still see this so differently? I wonder if there's an experience you remember having that really impacted your views on this."
- If you're talking about critical race theory, you might say, "What is the most important thing you learned about race in school?"

- If you're talking about social welfare programs and how much money should be invested in them, you might say, "How have you thought about some of the toughest times in your life? Where have you received the most help? When you haven't received much help, how has that impacted you?"

Parent-Child Relationships Are Filled with Unspoken Expectations

We have another set of usually unarticulated expectations around why we create families in the first place. It's changed dramatically over time. Both our motivation for having families and our expectations of roles within families have shifted from biological imperative and economic necessity to something more like self-fulfillment and the creation of idyllic childhoods. We're not looking for help on the farm or in the family store; we're sorting out our deep-seated stuff while packing healthy lunches, planning Pinterest-worthy birthday parties, and developing assertive but kind human beings.

In *All Joy and No Fun: The Paradox of Modern Parenthood* (the parenting book Sarah recommends to all new parents), Jennifer Senior details how children went from being seen as essential farm labor or apprentices in the nineteenth and early twentieth century to *parents* being essential to their children's overall happiness. Senior quotes sociologist Viviana A. Zelizer, who describes today's children as "economically worthless but emotionally priceless."[4] We keep amping up our expectations around the emotional bonds between parents and their children, which we seem to believe are created by parental attention.

A 2016 study quantified this shift. Researchers found that between 1965 and 2012 mothers doubled the time spent with their kids, despite the fact that millions of women joined the workforce and should in theory have less time than ever. Fathers today quadrupled the amount of time spent with their children as compared to the fathers of 1965.[5] No one parenting young children today needed the study to explain the intensity of modern parenting, including the meta aspects: "We seem to be parenting in a more intense way. Is that good or bad? Are we being too intense about our intensity?"

Changes in caregiving from one generation to another are usually better understood by examining societal trends than interrogating individual choices. That doesn't stop us from interrogating ourselves and each other and taking those interrogations personally. Parents of adult children might find themselves confused by the passion their children—now parents themselves—bring to screen time rules and nutritional guidelines when they were never concerned by such things. Different approaches in everything from educating children to faith formation can trigger feelings of judgment and disrespect in families. If a daughter makes enormous sacrifices to breastfeed, how should her own mother feel about her choice to formula feed? When we choose a different method of discipline than our parents', are we implicitly critiquing their methods? Parents of grown children say they only want their children to be happy, but what if those same children find happiness only in rejecting the choices of their parents? What we say and what we expect when it comes to parenting are very far apart.

These stealth expectations pave the way for resentment before political conflicts ever enter the picture. Those of us raising little humans and investing in every aspect of their development can be righteously indignant about our parents' relative indifference to how their votes, opinions, and media habits affect us. When we are consumed by how every tiny choice reflects on us as parents, how can our own parents seem so immune to how their choices affect us? We can't free ourselves of all the forces that create different expectations among our family members. We *can* try to see them, label them, and keep them in mind when we're responding to conflict so that when political conflict does enter the room, we are more prepared.

Making the Connection

One way to reveal stealth expectations is to put the verbal equivalent of floodlights on them:

- "Mom, I know that you worked so hard to breastfeed me and that breastfeeding is really important to you. I want you to know that I don't take any of that for granted, and I want to honor the way that you parented me. I'm just choosing a different way of feeding my baby. I've looked at the research and thought hard about what works in our lives. This is not a criticism of what you did or a lack of appreciation for it. I just want you to hear from me that we're going in a different direction because of where we are in our lives right now."

- "I know you expected your mom and me to stay together. It's hard to see us divorce when you're in your late twenties, and I can imagine that it makes you wonder if parts of your childhood were a lie. I want to promise you that they weren't. Every memory you have of us as a family is a real memory. We loved each other and you more than we can say."

- "Pop, I know that you don't like it when I disagree with you. I want you to understand how much I respect you. My disagreement is not disrespect—it's the opposite. I know how hard you've worked in your life and how smart you are. I love you so much. I just see this differently than you do, and it's important to me that you hear that. It hurts that we disagree, but I think we need to love each other enough to talk about it."

Allow for Complexities

Although we intellectually know that our family members are going to see the world differently, it is emotionally exhausting when they do. Our expectations of these relationships are enormous and constraining. They don't allow for the kinds of complexities that life is filled with: immigration status, illness or disability, economic stressors, tragedy, or a global pandemic.

Just as we bring asymmetrical expectations to the table about whether to fight about politics at all and how to fight if we do, we bring very different social context to our political dialogue. If you grew up in the age of Jim Crow, being told that an idea or statement is racist will most likely feel harsher and more personal than if you grew up singing along to "Everyone's a Little Bit Racist" from Avenue Q. If you grew up during the Kennedy administration, when presidential indiscretions were kept a secret, then you will have an experience with respecting the office that someone who grew up during the Clinton administration never had. If you grew up with Walter Cronkite telling almost all Americans the same news from a position of deep trust, then you will most likely feel overwhelmed by the flood of our current news media in a way that someone who grew up post-9/11 will never feel.

Despite the deep roots of our biology, most of us grow into very different people from our caregivers and siblings. That's what we're *supposed* to do. Raising a child is a creative act in every sense of the word. We are not reproducing ourselves. We're making new people, as different from each other as they are from us. No matter how loving, fun, lively, active, faithful, or idyllic the household is, the people who emerge from it are going to be their own people. And yet, even this idea reflects culture and historical context that will feel very foreign to many Americans.

When a child deconstructs or changes or abandons their faith, changes political parties, comes out, transitions, starts to process trauma, desires to be reunited with biological parents decades after adoption, or shifts in any other significant way, it can feel like rejection to their family members. These changes will probably involve a painful road for everyone. Abandoning or reexamining the fundamental identities of our childhoods is difficult emotional work made painful when our family members seem unable or even unwilling to support our journey—perhaps because their own journeys have taken them in such different directions.

As much as turning from home on any given topic can feel like failure, we hope to hold it as the natural evolution of human beings. If we are to continue to evolve, we need to allow those in our closest relationships to evolve as well. Our current state can become the focus of any evolution, but where we started is just as important. Seeing as clearly as we can where our family members started and how that set their expectations can help us see they might have a much harder road to walk before they can hear our perspectives with an open mind.

Making the Connection

If you're feeling strain in a relationship with a family member, it might be helpful to name the expectations you had for that person and what you've learned about them that disrupts those expectations.

- "I had always imagined that my sister's wedding would look just like mine. I've learned that's not what she wants for life. That doesn't mean she's rejecting my path. She's just on her own."
- "We dreamed that our son would love music the way our entire extended family does. But he's been telling us for a while that sports is where his passion lies. We've got to listen and let him lean into his own talents."

- "I expected that my partner would practice our shared faith for the rest of his life. I've learned that he is more interested in developing a set of ethics that aren't connected to religion. It will be interesting to understand where we find common ground in our different approaches."

Show Up Honestly

Understanding our expectations is essential. The next step is even harder: living with our differences also requires a release of control. Take deep breaths, y'all; none of us are "release of control" experts. Learning to give other people space is a lifelong practice that allows more grace for others and (bonus!) for ourselves.

Releasing control is how we're able to love each other through deep division, especially as the world tells us that conflicting identities make us enemies. It's easy to hear the drumbeat of political messaging that tells us the "other side" is the enemy. But often the "other side" loves us dearly, and we them. So how could they be our enemy?

To all the beautiful people who email us asking what to do about their loved ones who feel lost to internet conspiracies or political cults, we sometimes have to answer in a deeply unsatisfying way: the best thing is to stop doing and start being.

We cannot turn our family members into projects. We cannot shame and judge them or ourselves into seeing the world as we see it, voting as we vote, and engaging as we engage. We do not choose our families. We can only choose how we interact with them. When there is love and safety but serious disagreement, we can just keep showing up for each other lovingly anyway. We keep disagreeing. We go to the wedding. We send the birthday card. We organize the meal train during surgeries. We call. We text. We extend the dinner invitation. We have the political conversations and agree to talk again soon before moving on to when the next vacation is planned.

Separating from each other in our families and homes reinforces each "side's" worst beliefs about the other. If you are in a relationship where you are safe and secure (by which we mean that your fundamental identity is not being attacked, and you are not physically, emotionally, or financially threatened), it is worth considering how you can keep doing your work and showing up joyfully as your full self with your people. If you're not in a safe and secure relationship, please spend some time with us at the end of this book. We want to give you lots of resources, love, and encouragement.

We learned from Dr. David Campt, a guest on our podcast, that staying in relationships where we are safe can help us be better allies. Dr. Campt is the founder and principal of The Dialogue Company and creator of the White Ally Toolkit. He told us that if you are white and want to be part of antiracist work, you have enormous opportunities to influence other white people. America, he said, can be significantly more just if more white people merely acknowledge the reality of racism. That message can come through questions and connections, not just facts. People tend to double down on their beliefs when confronted with contrary facts. Dr. Campt urged us to "educate through experiences. Don't berate through facts."[6]

In order to invite that sense of connection through our experiences, we have to show up honestly. If we're hiding that we voted for "the other party," that we changed denominations or left the church, or that we support a certain policy, we can't be in real relationships with our siblings, parents, and caregivers. We have to work toward a culture in our families of recognizing each person's birthright to have different ideas and habits from each other.

We absolutely don't recommend that everyone "agrees to disagree." Instead, we recommend showing our beliefs instead of telling them, and showing the joy that accompanies our beliefs. Healthy perspectives, and the contentment that follow them, are contagious. And where they aren't . . . sometimes we just have to let that be. We can't argue people out of the existences that they want, even when those existences seem to make them some flavor of miserable.

"But but but . . . they live in an alternate reality." "They're so negative." "They adore this person I can't stand." "They make decisions I don't understand at all." "They say terribly hurtful things about people I love." These are real protests, and we respect them. We each have to weigh what we can handle in our lives carefully. We also have to know and be honest about the fact that deciding to be in long-term relationships of any kind, with anyone, for any reason means signing up for some amount of hurt. We will all disappoint and be disappointed in every context, and sometimes that disappointment will fill us with grief.

We want to be realistic. You might keep showing up patiently and lovingly for a lifetime and never feel that deep sense of connection you desire with your loved ones. For

reasons as varied as the human experience, we have different capacities to love and connect with each other. Even in
our most challenging familial relationships with people who
rarely show love, affection, or even something approaching
enthusiasm, we find that seeking that connection is worth our
energy. We learn so much about ourselves in the process. We
set an example for others, and we occasionally see glimpses
of the other person that are beautiful.

We also recognize that sometimes we cannot stay present
with each other through deep division. Sometimes the presence of trauma, abuse, addiction, or discrimination requires
us to part ways with our families of origin. We'll discuss this
unbearable sadness at the end of the book, and we want you
to know that if this is your reality, you are not alone.

We don't have a magic formula for knowing when to keep
working on relationships in families of origin and when to
distance. We do know that the presence of sustained conflict within families over politics necessitates support—from
partners and friends, coaches, clergy, and many times from
professional therapists. We think support from professionals
is critically important. Whether we're remaining in strained
relationships or exiting toxic ones, it's vital to incorporate
those wounds into a larger understanding of ourselves. Analyzing the role expectations play in our families of origin is
invaluable and can help us strengthen the connections in
other areas of our lives as well.

Moment OF **HOPE**

We frequently talk about HBO's documentary *The Vow* about Nxivm, a group that began by offering self-help courses and devolved into a misogynist cult. It depicts Catherine Oxenberg's persistent struggle to keep showing up for her daughter, India, who became deeply immersed in Nxivm to the point of isolation from her family. Catherine challenged India's perspective and fought to expose Nxivm's conduct for years. She also loved India. She tried to call her daughter even when she wouldn't answer. Catherine responded any time India reached out. She just kept being there, and eventually, she and India meaningfully reunited.

We love Catherine's example of lovingly showing up anyway. It's a reminder that even in extreme circumstances, where there is physical and psychological separation from each other, reuniting is an option. We also love that Catherine's example is both kind and honest. She neither shamed India nor endorsed Nxivm. Her actions over a span of years said to her daughter, "I love you. This is not good for you. It is not true. When you're ready to come home, I'm here."

NOW *What?*

We know our podcast listeners love to keep asking hard questions and that many readers do too. As you continue to shine a light on unexplored aspects of your family of origin, consider these questions:

- What's a historical event your parents experienced that's hard for you to fathom? What historical event shaped you of which your siblings or children will have no memory?

- Consider how you've observed conflict in your family. Who taught you how to have a fight and still love each other? How would your other family members answer that question? What are the unspoken rules about conflict in your family?

- Where have you made choices that are very different from your family? Did you move somewhere new? Become the first person in your family to attend college? Do you raise your children outside of a faith that was fundamental to your upbringing? How might your family be experiencing those choices?

- What are practical ways you can show up for a beloved family member in the midst of tension or conflict? Can you share a memory through a note or photo? Can you reconnect through a mutual interest in books or animals or a hobby?

- With whom in your family might you be able to discuss these questions?

2

The Families We Create

We Are More Than Our Opinions about Julia Roberts

Beth: My friend Brenda gave me a fabulous bridal shower. It wasn't surprising. Her home and wardrobe constantly revealed her acute sense of style and detail. Every aspect of the shower was perfect and made me feel so loved going into my wedding. The surprise of the day came when Brenda asked all the shower guests to write down a piece of advice for me. I read through lots of lovely sentiments—all heartfelt, kind, and wise in their ways. But one piece landed differently with me than the others. Gwen Mathews, a college administrator-turned-friend, wrote something like: "You must have friends. Your husband cannot be your best friend. That's too much pressure for one person."

Gwen stopped me in my tracks. I fell hard and fast for Chad Silvers, and he was very rapidly becoming my best friend. That became more true as I allowed my work as a new associate in a law firm to absorb most of my waking hours and nearly all my thoughts. It became even more true when we had our first baby, and my life was feed the baby, work, pump breast milk, work, pump while working, fret about both pumping and working, rush home, feed the baby, collapse, and repeat. I barely knew myself and lost touch with many friends who I adored. Chad had to fill that void. And Gwen was right, it was too much pressure for one person.

Fourteen years later, I can see clearly that my marriage is at its best when we're both taking good care of our friendships. Gwen tried to save me the lessons along the way. I guess sometimes we just have to learn for ourselves.

....

The prescient advice-giver at Beth's shower gave voice to something so many of us have observed. We put a lot of pressure on our partnerships. Our partners have to be our entire reason for being and our best friend (not to mention, know how to load the dishwasher the proper way, remember our every preference from TV to room temperature, oh, and be able to read our moods and respond perfectly to those moods no matter what's going on with them!). Even the smallest level of conflict puts more pressure on the relationship. When everyone already feels like they're living in a powder keg, the presence of political conflict can feel like someone lit a match.

It hasn't always been like this. Please indulge our inner history buffs for a moment; we find that thinking about where relationships started opens a window into better understanding our present.

Partnerships have always been fraught for very different reasons. Thousands of years ago, humans partnered
to meet basic needs for shelter and safety and reproduc-
tion. Hundreds of years ago, kingdoms rose and fell based
on the melding of families through marriage and the exchange of property and power that accompanied them. One
has to believe the fifth wife of King Henry VIII, his *second*
wife named Catherine, felt quite a deal of pressure on her
wedding day. That pressure was well placed because she
also became the second wife to lose her head. But even
beyond powerful rulers, sociologists have described marriages in agricultural societies as practical institutions that
were essential to the welfare of the family and stability of
the community.

With industrialization, there was suddenly less farming
and more wage labor and our home lives and work lives
began to separate. Partnerships became about choice and self-
expression. If we choose to marry, we're part of a long line
of people increasingly looking to our spouses to meet all our
physical, psychological, and emotional needs. Psychologists
at Northwestern University and the University of Chicago call
this the suffocation model of American marriage.[1]

We're also living in an era when more people can marry the
people they'd like to, and more people choose not to marry.
Long-term romantic partnership is no longer a given. Long-
term partnerships with beloved friends are becoming even
more prevalent. These partners buy houses, take vacations,
and entrust each other with their medical and financial care,
all grounded not in romance but in friendship. We love this
shift toward partnerships with defined purposes and the

accompanying understanding that we can't and don't need to be all things to each other.

People choose partners for all kinds of reasons. We've learned it's a mistake to assume much of anything about partnerships. When we're asked for advice about long-term committed relationships, we start with lots and lots of questions. We know that our own partnerships are quite different—not only because of the differences in personalities and dynamics, but also because we look to our partners for different things.

These differences show up clearly for the two of us when we travel. Sarah and Nicholas are in frequent contact, and Sarah puts Nicholas on speaker to dissect the events of the day with us. Beth and Chad give each other lots of space while they're on the road, checking in to say good morning and good night and then catching up in person after the trip. It's a small example of the significant differences in what we're looking for in our partners, and it's a gift to be able to observe these differences. Knowing there are lots of ways of being in partnerships helps alleviate some of the pressure on our own.

Making the Connection

If you're currently in a partnership, consider why. That sounds almost comically simple, doesn't it? Trust us! We think there's a lot of richness in unpacking it.

If you're not currently in what you would consider a partnership, consider your closest connections. What role do these relationships play in your life?

We Create Patterns without Thinking about Them

In any partnership, we look for some sense of satisfaction. We find each other to meet each other's needs. That sense of satisfaction can be disturbed and shored up a million times over in the course of a day. In our partnerships, we create patterns around belonging that either serve us well or compromise nearly every other realm of our lives. And because our brains are busy keeping our hearts pumping, remembering to pay the cable bill, and planning what we're going to wear tomorrow, among millions of other simultaneous functions, we're usually creating those patterns without giving them much thought. It's difficult to remember that much of what transpires between partners is not reflecting conscious decision-making.

The glance of annoyance over where she put the milk? It wasn't an intentional choice; it had more to do with the morning's tense work call than the milk.

The sharp tone when he asked what they wanted for dinner? It reflected exasperation that had been building all day and suddenly spilled over.

We are working out the entirety of our lives via interactions in our homes, and so is every other person within our household. Within the layers of relatively minor encounters, we're constantly communicating and receiving messages about how fully our partners are embracing us. As the pressure on the relationship increases, relatively benign differences of opinion can feel hurtful. When our partners don't agree with our opinions, it can feel like they don't agree with who we are.

Sarah: For the first decade of our marriage, Nicholas and I fought about the same thing. If I listed the topics, it wouldn't seem like we were fighting about the same thing but, trust me, we were. One of our first real fights was about the amount of empathy we should feel for celebrities, specifically Julia Roberts. The fight ended with Nicholas insisting that one could feel only a finite amount of empathy and shouldn't spend such a scarce resource on rich and famous people. (An argument I still find so ludicrous I am thrilled to have sealed it for all time in print to show our grandchildren and great-grandchildren!) We fought about money, specifically that he felt I spent too much and on the wrong things. We fought about sex and how to celebrate holidays and where to go on vacation and who was doing more chores. But what we were really fighting about is how I felt when Nicholas disagreed with me.

If he disagreed with my opinion, I felt like he was disagreeing with who I truly was. If he saw how upset I was by his disagreement and then continued to disagree with me, I felt like he didn't love me. The truth is I stuck up for Julia Roberts not just because I was defending empathy but because I was a complete devotee of her romantic comedies and romantic comedies as a genre, which had taught me that my marriage was supposed to make me better and shouldn't that feel good? (After all, I have seen Tom Cruise tell Renée Zellweger she completed him one million times, and they both seemed so happy!) Feelings drove the plot in all my favorite films. Richard Gere felt sad being away from Julia in *Pretty Woman*, so they got back together. Julia felt lost before marrying Richard Gere in *Runaway Bride*, so she ran before finding her egg preference and returning! Feelings were the only data I was taught to pay attention to, so

I learned to overidentify with them instead of looking for other input beyond how I felt in the moment. On top of it all, I tried to control Nicholas's reactions to my feelings.

....

When we're creating our families of choice, emotions should obviously play a role. We're not advocating for a return to dowries. Intense feelings of love or devotion or even sexual and platonic chemistry are going to continue to play a major role in the formation of our partnerships. And while these feelings will always play the starring role in romantic comedies, real life requires us to move beyond the meet-cute and final embrace. Emotions cannot be our only guide in conflicts, whether we're debating big moves or who should be on the Supreme Court or dishwasher loading. (In case you couldn't tell, Sarah feels there is a way to properly load a dishwasher. Beth vehemently disagrees. See? Conflicts are present in every type of partnership!)

Making the Connection

Consider an interaction that you had with your partner or someone significant in your life today. What was on your mind during that interaction? What do you think you communicated through it?

Now try standing in their shoes, bringing as much creativity as you can to fill in gaps in your knowledge. Occasionally practicing this exercise can make us much more gracious about tone of voice, body language, lapses in how closely someone is listening to us, and even the dishwasher situation.

Emotions Are Relevant but They Are Not Reality

Perhaps the greatest counterbalance to the giant pile of pressure heaped upon our partnerships by shifting culture (and romantic comedies—sorry, Julia!) is the work of Gary Chapman. In 1992, he wrote *The Five Love Languages: How to Express Heartfelt Commitment to Your Mate* and named acts of service, gift-giving, physical touch, quality time, and words of affirmation as ways we show love to one another. More than naming and classifying the love languages, it was the idea that even if we don't feel love, it is not that the love is not present—it's that we simply don't have the tools to properly see it. So often our partners are showing us love in their own way, which is a combination of gender, personality, family history, and cultural expectations. We feel unloved because our partner is offering an act of service when all we were looking for was physical touch. The reverse is also true. If we want our partners—romantic or platonic—to feel love, then we must speak in their love language.

Beth: I was sitting in an oversized chair on my second visit with my therapist when he leaned forward and said, "Well, Beth, as a 2 on the Enneagram, you're going to feel this hurt." I had literally no idea what he was talking about. If you're an Enneagram person (and as I've learned, the Enneagram people are very serious about the Enneagram), you hopefully remember how difficult the orientation is to nine different ways of being in the world. We eventually sorted out what my 2-ness represents, and it's been helpful.

More helpful to my relationship with Chad, who cannot roll his eyes hard enough at the mention of the Enneagram, has been understanding the subtypes. Since nine different ways of being in the world can't completely capture the complexity of the human experience, there are more layers! (The Enneagram people rejoice!) Subtypes, as I, not-really-an-Enneagram-person, understand them, describe three driving and mostly unconscious instincts underlying our behaviors. We all have three basic instincts: self-preservation, which is focused on physical safety, financial security, and comfort; one-to-one or sexual, which focuses on the energy created by intimate relationships; and social, which focuses on bonding with groups and communities. One of these three instincts, or subtypes, tends to dominate and be reflected in our behavior.

Over hours of conversation with my therapist, I learned that the one-to-one subtype is dominant for me. I want an intense connection. I want to stare into Chad's eyes and think deep thoughts together. Chad's dominant subtype is self-preservation. He wants me to stare into his eyes while considering the terms of our mortgage. I've joked many times that our conversations sound like this:

Beth: Why do you think we're here?
Chad: I don't know, babe. Can you be sure to use the AmEx at Kroger this week? It's 3x fuel points!

....

Whether we're using the Enneagram or Love Languages, learning to see our partners more clearly, instead of depending on how we were feeling at any given moment, has been enormously helpful for both of us. We became better versed at responding to our emotions instead of purely reacting. (Was I hurt because I was actually feeling underappreciated at work? Was I upset or was I just exhausted?) And as we did that for ourselves, we also got better at offering the same grace to our partners. When our emotions were leading the way, the only tool at our disposal was brute force control of both ourselves and our partners. Emotions are what they are—trying to control them is a recipe for disappointment with ourselves, much less with our partners whom we definitely cannot control. When we stopped trying to control our emotions, we found more space to observe them and respond accordingly. Instead of feeling tossed by the winds of every mood, we were slowly (even in the middle of a storm) building navigational tools. (We're writing in past tense here like we've really nailed it. Please know that these are still aspirational thoughts! We're improving, and we will be practicing these skills until the end of our days.)

Making the Connection

If you feel like you and your partner are miles apart while sitting in the same room, try exploring the pressures you each feel inside the relationship (preferably during a relaxed time when no one is hungry or tired!).

- "I realize we all get so many messages about what marriage is supposed to be. I value this relationship and I want to get it right, but I also don't want to add to the pressure we already feel."
- "It feels like we're ships passing in the night right now. I know you've been really busy, and I totally

support everything you're doing. I just miss being friends in addition to being roommates."

- "I hate feeling like I've disappointed you. Maybe we could talk about what we both expect when we visit each other's families."
- "The beginning of our relationship was so exciting. I feel the pressure to keep that level of emotional excitement all the time, and I wonder if we're both feeling the strain of that."
- "What's your favorite romantic comedy, and how did it mess you up?" (Kidding! . . . kind of.)

If fights over Julia Roberts can leave us battling over how to control each other (and each other's emotions), it is not surprising that political conflict inside a partnership is particularly fraught. We feel our partners should be on the same page with us about everything—after all, we *chose* each other. If conflict over leaving clothes in the dryer can increase that pressure, how much harder will conflict over issues of identity or voting or politics be?

Is Our Conflict a Strength?

We would love to hold up partners like James Carville, a Democratic strategist and commentator, and Mary Matalin, a Republican strategist turned Libertarian, as proof that love triumphs over political differences. But we know that relationship because it is an exception, not the rule. Political polarization in both platonic and romantic partnerships is well-documented, and social media and relationship apps help us sort by like-mindedness with ever-increasing efficiency.

Even in relationships where we're generally on the same page, political conflict can rear its head. We wonder if that kind of political conflict, between people who generally agree with each other, can be even more painful. We talked in chapter 1 about how much it hurts when we disappoint each other's expectations. When we expect our perspectives to align and they don't, it hurts.

Beth: I basically blew it in my marriage during the 2020 election. I had spent months arguing in public and at home that in this particular election, it was important to vote for Democrats. I believed (I still think correctly) that the election was less about policy and more about ensuring that our government could continue to function democratically. Neither Chad nor I had ever previously been Democratic voters, but I felt that the moment, rather obviously, required it.

So I was surprised and dismayed as we drove home from the polls to learn that Chad had voted for the Libertarian Party in nearly every race. I'm not going to lie to you. It felt like a gut punch. I felt disrespected. I felt like Chad must not value my expertise and my work. I was mad at him.

And he was mad at me for being mad at him (partnerships are fun like that!). He felt like I was being controlling. He was right about that. He wanted space to vote however he wanted. He wanted me to respect his thought process even though I strongly disagreed with it.

It was tense around our house for a good long while. It was a weird period of time. Chad and I are so aligned about the big things, so accustomed to being different about the little things, and so good at laughing about our conflicts (we have a yearslong argument about René Descartes and ceiling fans that makes us both laugh until we cry at least once every winter). It surprised me how much it hurt that we voted differently.

We broke that tension by walking through what we felt: You're mad. I'm mad. We're both allowed to be mad. It also doesn't have to mean more than that. We don't have to change anything. Nothing is broken. This one just stung.

....

Breaking down what's happening is a useful tool and one that we don't use enough. It's easy for conflict to balloon. It's easy for "You disappointed my expectations with your vote" to turn into "WHAT ELSE DON'T I KNOW ABOUT YOU? WHERE ELSE ARE YOU DISRESPECTING ME?" We can make our political differences mean more than they mean in a hot second. An argument about household chores can become a stand-in for relationship pressure. And an argument about politics can quickly become an argument about, well, everything else we might want to argue about. (Beth offers here a plug for her sense that there is not, in fact, one correct way to load the dishwasher, and her sense that making room for alternative loading methods is highly relevant to making room for conflicting political opinions.)

When we break down what's actually happened and how we feel about it, we can consciously decide that it doesn't have to mean more. Sometimes it's really as simple as: "You disappointed my expectations. I'm mad. You're mad that I'm mad about that. I'm mad that you're mad that I'm mad.

We're allowed to feel these feelings." This technique isn't a magic elixir. It can still be very uncomfortable to recognize serious variances in how we see the world. It is very uncomfortable to ask what those variances mean.

It is uncomfortable, but discomfort is different from and does not have to equal disdain.

> **Discomfort is different from and does not have to equal disdain.**

If we can work out how we feel and live through the discomfort, it's possible to stay in relationships—even to grow in them. In fact, the most growth we've experienced in our closest relationships has come from very uncomfortable moments.

This isn't always the case. Beth and Chad reached different conclusions about candidates based on fairly minor disagreements about style and governance. Even fairly minor disagreements can become fertile ground for real battle. Every message we receive politically raises the stakes of conflict. Maybe we agree with our partners about the need to take care of the planet but disagree about who should primarily do that and how. Maybe we agree with our partners that everyone should have access to high quality health care but we part ways on how to pay for that care. These differences can exist among people who affiliate with the same political party and vote for the same candidates, and they still feel overwhelming. They also represent much more than political discord.

─ *Making the Connection* ─────────

Consider the last argument you had with your partner or a very significant person in your life:

- How might you break down what happened? We just want to be factual here. In simple sentences that both of you would agree with, what went down?
- Now, go back through those simple statements and label your corresponding emotions. This is your chance to say how you felt about what happened.
- When you break it down this way, does it make the conflict seem more or less important? What can you learn from it?

Sarah: Nicholas and I are both Democrats and have been since we began dating in college. At the time, we had lots of rousing debates about feminism and the war in Iraq and which candidate could win which election, because that's what you do in college. You have rousing intellectual debates that have lots of room to spread out. As we got older, we still agreed on the big things, but our disagreements over the small things took on a certain edge. We had fewer arguments about policy and philosophy and more arguments about strategy. Most of them involved Nicholas being much more cutthroat when it came to Republicans than I was. He's a pessimist (and a 6 on the Enneagram), so he defaults to the worst in people and the worse outcome. I'm an optimist (and a 1 on the Enneagram), so his catastrophizing feels like an attack. Even after all this time and

practice teaching myself that his disagreement is not a judgment on me, when the stakes are high in a political argument,
I find myself feeling very angry and very disrespected and very
righteous (my favorite emotion!).

....

    Sarah and Nicholas aren't the only couple arguing from
differing personalities as much as substance. It happens to
the two of us (Sarah and Beth) in our work. As we write this
chapter about partnerships, we're having a running disagreement *inside the pages of this book* about whether there is one
correct way to load a dishwasher (in case you didn't notice).
We don't even share a dishwasher! This conflict is a reflection of our personalities. If you'll forgive another Enneagram
reference, Sarah is a 1. She's convinced that there is always
a correct way and that the real journey in life is to find that
correct way and enthusiastically adopt it. Beth is a 2. She's
far more concerned about everyone feeling comfortable and
appreciated for loading the dishwasher than with the direction of the plates. (And in her unhealthy moments, she'll load
the dishwasher herself and put the dishes away while they're
piping hot so no one has a chance to criticize her dishwasher
skills, and everyone will love how helpful she's been.)

    Dishwashers aside, understanding the Enneagram and
Love Languages (and Gretchen Rubin's *The Four Tendencies*
and John Gottman's the Four Horsemen and a million other
insights we've collected over the years) has been helpful in
both our life partnerships and our business partnership. They
are useful tools because they all help bring clarity to our personalities and underlying motivations. We love understanding

what fundamentally drives us and each other in our most stressful moments.

Let's face it. We experience a lot of our most stressful moments with our partners. Our partnerships are the places where we're likely to default to our most basic patterns. Having a bit of shorthand to help us understand and observe what's happening helps.

Of course, even with the best tools, some partners experiencing political differences find their disagreement ballooning beyond political candidates and tactics. As COVID-19 exposed, our political parties are shaping views about tangible, behavioral, consequential aspects of our everyday lives. If one person in a partnership became a devoted mask-wearer who rarely left home while the other person believed that concerns about transmission were exaggerated or fabricated, it was difficult to bridge that gap.

The rubber met the road in these partnerships as people found themselves negotiating the "rules" for leaving the house. The consequences were sometimes greater than broken trust, as partners contracted COVID-19 and transmitted it in their households. Couples battled over decisions about whether to send children to school. Roommates struggled over decisions concerning indoor dining, work environments, and vacations.[2] These conversations all took place during the existential and constant stress of the pandemic, which made them weightier for partners.[3]

COVID-19 filtered through the lens of political partisanship caused some partners to feel that they were in different universes. Alternate realities are also causing some partnerships to break under the weight of political cult theory. When one partner takes in information from sources their partner doesn't consider credible, even the most seasoned practitioner of grace finds it difficult to move forward.[4]

Political differences can also surface fundamentally different values around race and equity. Partners have shared with us stories of challenging conversations about privilege. Listeners of color and readers who have immigrated to the United States, especially when partnered with white people who were born and have always lived in America, have shared with us that their partners can be dismissive of structural, racist obstacles. White male partners have expressed feeling devalued by discussions about the need to center women's perspectives and the perspectives of people of color. Where partners come from different socioeconomic backgrounds, prejudices and insensitivity can be harshly felt. We've heard from people struggling to help their partners see the destructive and ever-present consequences of white supremacy. These topics are introducing real and significant conflict into partnerships, increasing already substantial pressure on the relationship.

We recognize that political disagreements are not hypothetical and that sometimes political disagreements move out of the realm of opinion. When the difference isn't obvious, we try to step back and ask this question: "Is the space between us right now the result of characteristics that, in another context, we'd view as a strength of our relationship?" If so, we think it's worth it to investigate what we can learn from the conflict and to build on that strength within our partnership. If not, we think it warrants further evaluation. We talk more in the note at the end of this book about that further evaluation. For now, we want to say clearly that no one should be degraded in any relationship, and especially not in the relationship that should provide the most trust, love, and support.

In our own partnerships, we see themes emerging in our central conflicts. Both of our partners are more focused on money than we are. After years of work, we can see that prioritization isn't because our husbands value our family's financial security, and we don't—rather, it is a reflection of personality (compounded by family history and cultural messages). Both of our partners are more focused on our kids' academic successes, while the two of us focus more on our kids' emotional intelligence. These approaches lead to conflicts but not because one person cares about the kids and one doesn't. Again, our partners are just different than we are. Both of our partners tend to focus on the exercise of political power—Nicholas favors using it; Chad favors restricting it. Compared to our husbands, we both seem like political pacifists. We think this, too, is healthy and good for our relationships.

Seeing ourselves and our partners more clearly takes practice and patience and vulnerability. We're not picking winners and losers when it comes to personality traits. We don't want to see our own limited perspective with clarity just so we can announce it is the superior approach. We want to take in the breadth and diversity of approaches inside our partnerships because there are different strengths in different strategies. Surviving life with another person takes the resilience and adaptability of both people. Especially when you add more people to the mix.

NOW *What?*

If you're currently in a partnership:

- Consider what expectations you had of the other person when you entered into the partnership.
- What have you learned about those expectations since you entered the partnership? Have you adjusted your expectations to match what you've learned? If not, how might you do that?
- When you think about conflicts with your partner, what personality traits do you see coming into play? Are themes surfacing?
- Do you see any strengths of your relationship in those themes?

If you're not currently in what you consider a partnership:

- What personality traits come into play in most of your close relationships?
- How can you frame those personality traits as strengths that you bring to your relationships?
- What do you notice about personalities that complement yours well?

3

Raising Citizens

"Everything's Going to Be All Right" and Other Lies We Tell Kids

Sarah: I vividly remember the first time one of my children asked about death. My firstborn son, Griffin, was sitting at the kitchen counter having a snack. He was probably three or four. A dear friend of mine had recently passed away. I hadn't told him explicitly what was happening, but he had clearly figured out that something was going on. He then explained to me that he was never going to die. I took a deep breath.

"No, sweetie, that's not true. Everyone dies. You will die. Amos will die. I will die. Daddy will die. Hopefully, this will not happen for a very long time, but everyone dies eventually," I told him.

My voice filled with emotion and my eyes filled with tears as I watched my firstborn's face crumple with sadness.

"But that makes me so sad," he said as he started to cry.

I didn't sugarcoat it. I didn't try to lessen the blow. I didn't launch into what happens after we die because, while I have faith, I don't have answers, and he was looking for answers. I placed the hard truth softly on the counter between us and let it sit there.

His tears grew more urgent, and so did mine. I picked him up and held him. There was nothing else to do or say. A minute or so later he squirmed out of my arms and ran off to play.

....

"Everything's going to be all right."

That's what we say to the children in our lives. It falls out of our mouths almost instinctively at the first sign of tears or sadness. As new parents, we swaddle our fragile infants and sway back and forth while shh-ing and cooing, "It's OK. I'm here." As caregivers, we scoop up stumbling little ones when they scrape their knees and assure them, "You're OK!" As teachers and mentors, we sit next to teenagers struggling with those first steps toward independence and desperately try to instill confidence, "It's going to be fine. You've got this!"

We speak it over and over like a mantra. We whisper it like a prayer. We say it as much to ourselves as to them.

Author Ellen Cantarow famously said, "Making the decision to have a child—it's momentous. It is to decide forever to have your heart go walking around outside your body."[1] She perfectly captures the vulnerability all of us feel when we look at the children in our lives. We invest so much in them. We invest our very selves in them through the currencies of genetics, time, money—our literal blood, sweat, and tears. We love them so much. We hurt when they hurt, and we desperately want them to be OK.

In sharp contrast, very few of us think assuredly, "Everything's going to be OK," when looking at the state of our world, national politics, or even our local paper. While having a child has always been an act of faith, a gamble on the future seems particularly risky in the twenty-first century. For over a decade, the American Psychological Association has conducted an annual "Stress in America" online survey of thousands of Americans of all ages.[2] When asked to consider our country's future, an overwhelming majority of all adults surveyed in 2020 (77 percent) said that thinking about America's future caused them stress, and the number of adults who feel stress about the future of our nation has risen every year. Younger generations, in particular, exhibited skyrocketing stress levels as a result of the disruptions to their school and social lives due to the pandemic. And if you look at the stress trends across generations, it is the millennial generation—the generation currently in peak childbearing years—who have consistently exhibited rising stress levels and report major increases as a result of the pandemic.

Our stress rises because we see their stress and struggle. We want to honestly tell the children we love that everything will be OK. Yet when we look around us at a global pandemic, rising partisan rancor, the threat of climate change, the growing gap between the rich and the poor, and crises in seemingly every single major societal institution, it feels like telling them that would be a lie.

Making the Connection

Wanting to soothe our kids and assure them their fears or anxieties or suffering will come to an end is a fundamental part of caregiving.

- Thinking back on when you were a kid, when did a trusted adult give you assurances that made you feel better? When did a trusted adult give you assurances that made you feel worse?
- What is a child in your life struggling with? Write down all your wishes (no matter how unrealistic) about how you wish this struggle will end.
- When did a child ask you a hard question and you had no idea how to respond?

Avoidance Is Not an Option

When the truth is hard, it's easy to dodge the conversation. But avoidance—or batting down kids' questions—is just another form of lying. The mythology surrounding the Kennedy family is that Joseph Kennedy, the patriarch of the family, would quiz his children about the latest headlines around the dinner table every evening. Today, the idea that you could contain the news environment in a newspaper headline that your children would have to seek out is laughable. (Plus, no one is trying to hold up ole Joe as a paragon of parenting!) Even a teacher wanting to quiz her students on news sources would need an auditorium full of kids in order to assign all the ways in which Americans consume news. From cable news to social media feeds to polititainment, all of us—including our kids—are inundated with everything from global issues like climate change to the latest political Tweetstorm.

It's the air we breathe in our hyperpolitical environment, and there is no way to keep kids from being exposed. They are listening to us, and they are also talking to one another. Anyone who has been around children remembers the moment when they were listening to children talk to one another and felt shocked to realize how much they pick up from adult conversations, including cuss words. (Sarah would like to place a formal apology to Felix's kindergarten teacher here.) They work out the questions we won't answer, the topics we avoid, and the values we exhibit with one another.

> **When the truth is hard, it's easy to dodge the conversation. But avoidance—or batting down kids' questions—is just another form of lying.**

Our kids are living in the same information age that we are. We need to abandon the idea that we can protect them from this environment.

We also need to abandon the idea that the best way to help kids address stressful news is to lean on our well-worn instincts of assuring them it will all be all right. If the pandemic has taught us anything, it's that we cannot and should not promise something we cannot deliver. We don't know how to solve climate change and mass incarceration. We don't know if our country will be able to face the challenges of a changing economy. We are also scared when we read the details of the latest school shooting, and we get mad when our friends disagree with us about how to address gun violence.

We know deep down—even as we're swaddling and placing Band-Aids and wiping tears—that our children will face political conflict at every stage of their lives. That is as true with politics as it is with peer relationships and academic challenges. We've learned from our kids that no one wants to be denied information. Denying information is not guarding a heart.

Instead, we all want to be invited into the conversation with grace and curiosity. We want to have our fears affirmed and our experiences heard. We want to be trusted with the tools to solve our own problems and contribute in a meaningful way. We don't want someone to tell us they have all the answers. Trust is built when someone admits they were wrong, not when they insist they have a monopoly on being right. We want others to trust us enough to say "I don't know" when that's the truth. We want to have our values acknowledged, and we want to feel supported by those around us.

Our kids are no different.

Beth: My parents talked about news and politics every day of my childhood. They weren't partisans; they were news junkies. I can close my eyes and smell the local newspaper sitting on a coffee table between my parents' recliners. They traded sections, reading it cover to cover before my dad would take it out with the garbage. As soon as cable news became a thing, it was on in our house during major events. I remember my parents glued to the Clarence Thomas confirmation hearings—how quiet they were, how frequently they sighed and shook their heads, how confusing the whole thing seemed to be for them. I remember watching OJ Simpson's Bronco chase. I remember President Clinton's impeachment in detail. I remember talking with them about Operation Desert Storm.

Mom and Dad intend to stay informed, and they always have. They taught me to witness world events, to try to be open to new information, to sense when history is unfolding. Because of that, I turn to them when the news becomes challenging. I trust the way they take in information because I watched their news habits every day of my childhood.

There Is No ONE Right Answer

When we invite our kids into the conversation, we're instilling both our political preferences and our political communication styles into their conversational blueprints. Whatever the dynamic in our relationships around politics, it can have risks and benefits for the children observing that dynamic. There is not one right way to have political conversation as adults (although there are some wrong ways!); therefore, there isn't one right example to show to our kids.

Some of our children are witnessing adults—friends, partners, relatives, etc.—in perfect alignment about politics. This can powerfully instill a sense of prioritization around values for them. The issues adults choose to discuss and the vocabulary they use to discuss those issues tell children what they think is important in the world and why.

Some of our children are witnessing adults in conflict. This shows our kids that conflict is inevitable among people who love each other. They learn that reasonable people can differ in their analysis. They learn about productive and unproductive styles of conflict—*even if* most of it is unproductive. This is important and necessary too.

Whether we're modeling lockstep agreement, constant opposition, or something in the wide range of options between those extremes, we can increase the value proposition for children around us by clarifying our roles in their political development. Caregivers and other adults who figure prominently in children's lives are always instilling values in children. Our politics, at their best, should be an application of our values.

Making the Connection

Think about what we're saying when we support a person, position, or party:

- My support comes from my belief in [statement of values].
- My support reflects the fact that I believe [statement of values] is more important than [competing concerns].
- My support reflects my willingness to accept [flaws in person, position, or party] because of the importance I place on [statement of values].

Imagine a child you love and a specific candidate you've supported. Try filling in these blanks to consider how you might share more of your thoughts with that child.

Even if we never break down our opinions concretely, the children around us will absorb those messages, because they are always smarter and more observant than we're giving them credit for. And we can celebrate that! We should be sharing what's important to us and why with our children.

Now, any of us who have spent time with legalistic tweens or teenagers (that charming characteristic is developmentally appropriate and also incredibly frustrating) know that it is very easy for these messages to morph into indoctrination and for our kids to morph into idealogues. Families have choices to make about how strongly they want to transmit political messages to their children, and much of that decision-making will shift over the course of our kids' lives. We're not here to advocate for a particular intensity. In fact, we take different approaches to this in our own families.

Sarah: Considering the title of our first book, I'm a little embarrassed to admit that when politics comes up with my kids, I probably do more talking than listening. It's not that I'm not interested in their perspective or don't want to fully understand their questions, I do. But I'm raising three boys and there's a part of me that feels like my role as their mother isn't to empower their voices. Society is going to do a fine job of teaching them that, as men, they have something to say. I feel like it's important for me to teach them that women have something to say too. Specifically, I want them to understand women have lots to say about politics. I want them to see politics as women's work as much as men's. I want them to see a woman's expertise in politics as natural and unsurprising. After all, as I'm constantly reminding my other male relatives, I do have expertise. I have a law degree and worked in the United States Senate. I ran for elected office and served a term on my city commission. I spend hours every week reading the news and offering political commentary on our podcast. I don't teach my boys that this level of expertise is required. They still have lots of political opinions, and I take them seriously. But I do teach them that level of expertise should be respected, even—scratch that—*especially* when it comes from a woman.

Beth: When Jane and Ellen ask me questions, as they do constantly about everything, I become the annoying parent who responds with another question. I remember several years ago when Jane heard a kid on the bus say that Hillary Clinton likes to kill babies. Jane had no idea what he was talking about, and I was so glad she asked me. I explained the political question in the best language I could find for her: "Some people think that parents and doctors should decide whether to have a baby. Some people think that once a family is pregnant, they should be required to have the baby." And then I asked her, "What do you think?"

We did "What do you think?" again when the girls listened to a jury read its verdict in former Minneapolis police officer Derek Chauvin's trial. We did "What do you think?" multiple times during the COVID-19 pandemic, as the girls heard students arguing about masks, where the novel coronavirus originated, and how seriously we should be taking it. They've asked questions about school shootings, wildfires, transgender sports bills, and impeachment trials. I also do my best to lay out the facts and then turn it over to them to consider.

I don't withhold my opinion. I just invite them to share first. We're all honest. Sometimes we disagree, and it gives us a chance to talk about different values and how we handle it when those values lead us to different ideas. Very frequently, I tell them the hardest truth: I don't know.

Sometimes they'll ask a question that makes my stomach hurt, because I don't know the answer or because I don't want them to have to grapple with it yet or because it just feels too heavy in the moment. I'm learning to quickly move past that feeling to celebrate that they keep asking me. I'm learning to cherish the conversations we have together and the insight they develop through these discussions. I'm raising two girls who are developing independent, well-considered opinions and who can express those opinions assertively and authentically.

....

As much as our children's genders and societal expectations about those genders influence our approaches, we have to admit that our personalities are also at play. We're both leaning into our gifts as parents. Sarah is naturally gifted in connecting a topic to morality. She's a strong and passionate orator. She speaks with authority and conviction. She brings all these strengths to the table in educating her children about politics. Beth is naturally a gentle guide. She finds questions that draw out the best in people. She listens compassionately so that others feel safe to share their hearts with her. She brings these strengths to the table in interacting with her children.

There is not one right way to approach these conversations (this is the great news). We find that in talking politics with our kids, following our natural talents usually serves us well.

Making the Connection

We've developed different approaches to our kids' political questions based on their personalities and ours. What approach do you notice yourself taking today with the kids you love? How do you see your gifts at play in these conversations? How might you bring more of your gifts to the table?

You Don't Have to Be an Expert

Although we differ in how much we want to pass on our own positions to our children, we align on the goal of having political conversations with them: we want to raise citizens. Our children were all born in the United States, inheriting "citizenship" as their birthright. We want more than that. We want them to behave as more than just inhabitants of the country. We want them to be active participants, constantly securing and earning its privileges through the exercise of their responsibilities.

That might sound like overkill, especially if the most precious children in your life are barely crawling. But it's a useful framework for curious kindergarteners to young adults. We can support children in becoming citizens through so many relatively simple strategies—strategies that do not require us to become civics experts and that do not require us to check our own opinions at the door.

Anytime we interact with listeners and readers in person, we hear tremendous anxiety from adults about how to discuss politics with kids. Our exposure to experts around everything from breastfeeding to time-outs seems to have created a false sense that we need to have a PhD in psychology along with an LLM in international law in order to share our political opinions with kids without scarring them for life. We hear anxiety about having the right words to answer questions, explaining issues in developmentally appropriate terms, and ensuring that children don't discuss politics with friends in ways that will provoke conflict. These expectations

> **By virtue of being a loving adult to a child, you are qualified to talk politics with that child.**

are unrealistic and do not serve anyone—least of all the children in our lives.

By virtue of being a loving adult to a child, you are qualified to talk politics with that child.

In our experience, the best way to calm your own anxieties is to let the child lead:

- Pay attention to the child's questions and interests.
- Answer questions as directly and honestly as you can.
- Admit what you don't know.
- Allow the child to decide when the conversation is over. (Mercifully, they're almost always finished before we think we've even started.)
- Ask them what they think.
- When you don't know what to say, thank them for talking to you about it.

You don't need to be an expert; you need to be the kind of adult with whom a child wants to talk about important things again and again.

Raising citizens is about both conversation and action, and kids love to think about action. It's helpful to move the conversation beyond opinions and events to emphasize the actions we can take as citizens. Voting is an incredibly powerful act we take as citizens and the perfect way to show our kids that citizenship isn't just talking but *doing* as well. (Plus, there are stickers!) When it's available to you, take the children in your life to the polls. Sit them down at the table where you're voting by mail and discuss the ballot. Walk them to the mailbox as you send your ballot on its way. Talk to them about what is on the ballot and why.

We can also teach our kids that their voices matter long before they are eligible to vote. We can encourage them to write letters to their school faculty and to their elected officials. We can take them to school board and city council meetings. When they have ideas that would benefit the Scouts or the church worship service or the local YMCA, we can help them navigate the best channels to share those ideas. When we support our kids as they learn to contribute to their communities (and help them deal sometimes with disappointment in those spaces), we're helping them build powerful citizenship muscles.

Making the Connection

Make conversations about elections even longer in off-cycle elections. They'll hear plenty about presidential races, after all!

- Talk about congressional terms. Look up when your senators are up for reelection.

- Help them understand why we elect school board members and mayors and state representatives.
- Discuss the ballot referendum with them and ask for their opinions. (Californians, this might take you an entire semester, but we believe in you!)

Teaching Citizenship in a Community Classroom

There is so much pressure on those of us raising and loving little citizens—because of the stakes, because of cultural expectations, because we want so badly to emulate the best of our families of origin and perfect all their imperfections. The hardest part is that many of us are trying to do this all by ourselves. But citizenship is a group activity (we'll get into this in later chapters), so *raising* citizens cannot be a solo endeavor!

It's time to put down the expectation that only parents or designated caregivers should influence their children's political beliefs. Some of the best conversations we've had with our kids are when a trusted adult in their life expressed a political opinion different from ours. Suddenly, it's not so easy to lean on the crutches we use in our own lives to justify the political beliefs we disagree with. After all, we can't just look at our kids and say, "Grandpa is ignorant, just ignore him!" (Well, we suppose you can say that, but that's a conversation ender, not opener.) And it's not just political opinions our kids are exposed to that can teach them what it means to be a citizen. One of Griffin's Boy Scout leaders served in the National Reserves and that sparked a conversation about military service. Jane's church leader who is also an ecologist has profoundly influenced how Jane connects her care for the environment with her faith. When Sarah ran for city commission, the best part was getting her friends' kids involved with knocking on doors or walking in local parades. It showed them that elections were more than Facebook ads and ballot boxes. Jane and Ellen volunteer with Beth and Chad frequently, and they love hearing about Beth's board service for an organization that focuses on decarceration.

When we expand our children's vision beyond our nuclear family and beyond mere political debate, we show them in a more beautifully complex way that everything just might be all right. Not because we can assure them of a struggle-free future, but because we can assure them that whatever comes they won't be tackling that future alone. We show them that they are part of a community that cares about them and *for them*. We teach them they have a role to play in that future by showing all the ways our friends and families and neighbors do their part. We invite them to walk beside us as young citizens, no matter what the future holds.

NOW What?

- Around what topic do the kids in your life have a lot of anxiety? Can you allow yourself to listen and affirm that anxiety without trying to fix or solve it?
- Where do you feel limited in your political knowledge as a caregiver? What would happen if you just

admitted to your children that you simply don't understand the issue or don't know where you stand? Could you do the research together? Or maybe assign different positions to discuss the topic then switch?

- Is there a topic about which your child is particularly passionate? Could you reach out to someone in your community with experience in that issue—either through work or study or life experience? Can you trust that person and your child to influence each other without your input?

4

Friendships

Best Friends Forever . . . or Until We Disagree

Beth: The last time I remember seeing Sarah before we started our podcast was in 2005. We bumped into each other in the Phi Mu Chapter Room at a Transylvania University alumni reception. We had both gone to law school, and Sarah asked me what I was planning to do after graduation. I told her I had accepted a position at a Cincinnati law firm. "What about you?" I asked. "Are you heading to a firm?"

Sarah threw her head back and laughed, "Oh definitely not! Nicholas sold out so I wouldn't have to." And with that, I tried to smile and make my way toward a punch bowl.

....

Most friendships originate because of proximity, shared interests, a shared stage of life, and similar preferences. Our friendship is a study in almost the exact opposite dynamic. Despite being in the same sorority in college, we weren't close friends, and beyond Facebook, we did not stay in touch after graduation. And our few in-person interactions weren't exactly bonding—as evidenced by Beth's recollection of the alumni reception! As forty-year-olds, we can see that Sarah's extroversion complements Beth's introversion; that Beth's calm complements Sarah's passion; that Sarah's sense of free-dom complements Beth's intention to ensure that everyone is comfortable. In college, these differences were more pro-nounced, and we weren't exactly looking for close friendships that would work on us.

Beth reached out originally to ask Sarah about her home births and then realized we had a shared interest in politics. After Beth guest-posted on Sarah's parenting blog (where she would literally switch from stroller reviews to the Syrian civil war), we decided to start *Pantsuit Politics*. We knew there was a lot that connected us—we were both moms, we both had infants, we both had law degrees. And yet we were also pro-foundly aware of our differences. At first, the podcast was built around our different partisan affiliations. We started each show with "I'm Sarah from the left" and "I'm Beth from the right." (That's no longer the case, but that's a story for a differ-ent chapter!) We had (and still have) different ideas about the role of government and certain candidates. We had different emotional reactions to tough news stories—even where our opinions were perhaps the same. Sarah runs hot and easily expresses her anger and frustration. Beth can tap deep wells of calm and can articulate her sadness better than most. Our friendship thrives because of these differences, even as they present challenges that we have to work through.

Our early lives and adult existences are heavily shaped by our families of origin and the families we create. However, we belong not only to those who birthed us and brought us into the world but also to our first friend who chose us and shared our perspective. We experience the thrill of connection not only with the partner we chose to share major periods of our lives with but also with the best friend with whom we shared that one very intense phase. Sarah still thinks of her best friend from middle school, Heather, every time she sees a box of Pasta Roni, and Beth can't celebrate New Year's Eve without remembering slumber parties at her first best friend Katie's house. Friendships can define us and become an integral part of our stories.

We are driven from a very early age to reach out and connect—to *make* friends. Researchers have long pointed to the positive benefits of these connections for children. Strong social connections in kids and teens help build self-confidence and emotional resilience.[1] Every parent knows that a toddler making friends and a teenager prioritizing their friends are important developmental milestones. That's why parents schedule playdate after playdate and chauffeur tweens all over town. We know our kids need their friends.

We also know we need friends, and by the time we hit adulthood, we've made lots of friends through school or work. But then just as suddenly, it can feel like all the friends we've spent a lifetime collecting are in very different places than we are—from faraway physical locations to different life phases to politics that seem like a galaxy away from our own. What then? Do we work through our differences? Do we cut people loose? And if we do, how do we build new friendships around shared values?

Life Brings Us Together and Life Pushes Us Apart

We are told friendships are essential but given no tools or strategies to build those relationships or figure out what to do when those ties are tested. We don't even have great language to describe these relationships. We once bumped up against these linguistic limitations on our podcast after a listener pointed out that the word *girlfriend* becomes very confusing when used by women to describe their close friends and by gay women to describe their romantic partners. We thought *sister friends* might be a nice substitute, but where does that leave men when describing devoted friends? It leaves out close friendships held among men and women and nonbinary people. *Best friend* doesn't work when trying to define many close relationships, and it can feel a little juvenile. And *friend* by itself sounds so paltry. Beth has always loved *The Bob and Sheri Show*. The hosts describe each other as silver best friends and talk about their gold ones. Those titles feel closer to what we're going for, but we don't want to engage in a "Beloved Friends Olympics."

There is increasing understanding that, no matter the challenges friendships present, they are better than the psychological and physical and spiritual toll of loneliness. And we are living through an epidemic of loneliness. The Survey Center on American Life released a report in the summer of 2021 on the state of American friendship.[2] They found that over the past three decades Americans reporting they have *no* close friends has risen by a factor of five! Ten percent of men and fifteen percent of women report having no close friends. Human beings are not built for this. We are finely tuned social animals, evolved to depend on our fellow humans for safety and support. When we're alone, every anxiety is magnified and we feel particularly vulnerable. Even if being alone doesn't make us vulnerable to lion attacks anymore (at least in most parts of the world), that doesn't mean our amygdala knows the difference. As a result, our ability to self-regulate decreases, and our emotions can ride roughshod over our psyches and our health. Researchers at Brigham Young University looked at hundreds of studies on loneliness and its physical impact and found that it is as risky as smoking fifteen cigarettes a day or abusing alcohol.[3]

We need each other. So what's keeping us so far apart?

Most of us start early adulthood with close friendships formed during school. In high school and college, we have enough independence—and most importantly, enough support—to have the time and energy to make and build friendships. Even in the most intense academic environments, like graduate school, the stressful study environment usually creates bonds with fellow students.

Sarah graduated from both college and law school with several close girlfriends. Of course, almost immediately, these friends were scattered to the four winds with people pursuing jobs in other cities or getting married and following spouses to other states. While the academic structure literally keeps us and our friends in the same phase, real life can abruptly break us apart.

Sarah and her dear friend Elizabeth both got married after college graduation, but then Elizabeth had her first baby and Sarah went on to law school. Sarah's college roommate Erin stayed single for several years, as did her friend Catharine. Sarah and another friend, Aimee, decided to have kids at the same time, but Aimee had twins(!!!). They weren't studying for the same exams anymore. Fall vacations and spring breaks weren't scheduled on the same calendar. They were facing different challenges in different cities and felt very far apart.

Once she moved back to her hometown of Paducah, Kentucky, Sarah made friends with women who were in similar life phases and who often lived right around the corner. And yet even the seemingly unbeatable combination of proximity and shared experiences weren't enough to keep every connection strong.

Beth, true to that one-to-one Enneagram subtype, has had very strong friendships in every phase of life. She also has a strong sense of regret about the fact that those friendships have faded away with every life transition. She loves every person she's ever been close to, as much today as then. It's also true that she has not made the effort to stay in touch. She has unintentionally communicated that something else became more important than the friendship. She has allowed friendships to dissolve. This isn't an uncommon story, and if you share a version of it in your own life, Beth would encourage you to not feel guilty about it. We can know what we know only when we know it. What Beth knows now, to her very cells, is that friendships are lifelines. At this stage of her life, she is learning to prioritize friendship above nearly everything else. Her friends are integral parts of raising her children, keeping her motivated to work, ensuring that her marriage is healthy, and helping her make meaning in the world.

── *Making the Connection* ────────

Looking back over your life, what intense friendships have faded with time? Were there best friends with whom you spent every second to whom now you almost never speak?

What environments led you to bond quickly and intensely with new friends? What do those environments both share and not share with where you are now?

Friendships are easily built on the idea of shared perspectives and forged from that feeling of sameness. That's why finding friends inside an academic structure that literally groups us based on shared characteristics of age or interest or extracurricular experiences can make finding friends so easy. Plus, it trains us to believe that friends are friends *because* they are the same, which then becomes a bit of a self-fulfilling prophecy. Our friends are our friends because we feel the same about everything (or, at least, everything important), and if we run into differences, maybe it's because we shouldn't be friends.

Connection Comes from Conflict—Not Sameness

We were talking for hours every week through some of the toughest issues in America. We were connecting with one another and supporting one another and growing closer the whole time. And still the knowledge that we are very different people was always front and center. Sarah is an extrovert. Beth is an introvert. Sarah is a 1 on the Enneagram and feels zero responsibility for the emotions of others. Beth is a 2 on the Enneagram and feels profoundly responsible for the emotions of others. Sarah has never met a mic or camera she didn't love but hates small talk. Beth doesn't love the stage with quite the same passion but can connect with hundreds of people in a meet and greet line and remember each of their names and stories months later.

Our podcast thrives on this complementary dynamic. Our personality differences—not just our partisan disagreements—were something our listeners pointed to over and over again as a strength of our show. Some people needed to hear Sarah's rage. Some people needed to hear Beth's calm. Even listeners who strongly identified with one of us expressed surprise at how much they needed to hear the other's approach as well.

We were growing closer and closer outside of the show, especially as we traveled together. As we look back now, it is clear that we took great care with each other as our relationship grew. We couldn't lean on an intense phase of connection in which we were obsessed with each other's every thought. We couldn't lean on proximity—we live three hundred miles apart, so we weren't bumping into each other in the office or at the grocery. We knew not to make assumptions about each other. From the beginning, we knew our differences were many and that the relationship was being built on far more than our shared life experiences or similar interests.

The conflicts inside our friendship were inevitable, as they are in every friendship, but we had a different orientation to help guide us through it.

Between increased polarization and cascading crises, there are many opportunities for friendships to be tested. And that's just with regards to politics! There is also a universe of personal and personality-driven conflicts just waiting to surface inside every friendship, including but *certainly* not limited to talking too little, talking too much, dating choices, marriage choices, weddings, vacations, parenting strategies, differing life stages, even whether or not you're a citizen in Bachelor Nation. You don't realize you have a conflict with your friend until there's a sexual harassment controversy at the school your kids attend or you feel tension around birthday presents that reinforce stereotypes you'd rather leave behind.

For many of us the first signs that politics was revealing differences that perhaps had been there all along came in the wake of the 2016 election and grew over the next four years. Suddenly, friends we thought were on the same page as us felt like they were on different planets. That gap has seemed to widen with time.

We've heard from listeners who saw their personality differences with friends exacerbated and put on full display by the pandemic. Decisions about social distancing and masks created deep and personal wounds with layers of meaning attached to them. These wounds were especially pronounced for people who have or live with people who have risk factors that made them particularly vulnerable to severe cases of COVID-19. It was hard to watch friends disregard public health guidance without thinking, *Do they just not care about me?*

Even when we share the same politics, tension can enter the relationship when everyone is handling stress or crises in different ways and at different paces.

We each handle stressful situations in our own, very personality-driven way. As we began to travel together for the podcast, we saw this up close and personal. In the beginning, we shared hotel rooms so the care we were used to taking with each other during hour-long conversations across Skype was dialed up precipitously. As we navigated shared meals and shared bathrooms and long hours in front of crowds, we both felt the weight of all that care on top of the stress of live events and time away from our families.

Instead of worrying about upsetting each other, we needed to say the upsetting things out loud. In one particularly intense conversation on a highway in Iowa, we were both able to name how hard it was to be constantly navigating Sarah's hatred of small talk and Beth's need for solitude, to be making sure Sarah ate when she needed to and Beth had access to her Diet Coke, to be caring for each other while caring for ourselves and our audiences. In conversations like this, we find our hours spent in therapy helpful! We're able to say things like, "When this happens, I feel tense" and ask questions like, "What would be the most supportive thing I can do when you're feeling that way?"

We also decided, whatever the costs, we were done sharing hotel rooms! Somewhere along the way, we had internalized the idea that as females and as friends the most important thing was to eliminate all friction between us *on our own as individuals*. In actuality, we needed to name the friction and figure out how to let it live.

Making the Connection

- Where has friction reared its ugly head in your friendships?
- How did you deal with the conflict, if at all?
- Were you gentle with yourself in the face of this stress, or did you blame yourself and shoulder all the responsibility for fixing it?
- Do you have any friendships that survived intense conflict? What did you learn through that experience?

Letting friction live is our best advice in friendships. It's tempting to believe that friendships should be incubators of sameness. After all, we're choosing our friends—we don't *have* to be connected with them. And at a certain stage of life, friendship requires deliberate effort to stay in touch, to prioritize time for conversations and shared experiences. It's easy to think that we need to resolve tensions or walk away.

Friction that is allowed to live is a remarkable teacher.

But walking away deprives us of so much love, history, and perspective. It also deprives us of the chance to keep working on ourselves. Friction that is allowed to live is a remarkable teacher.

Sarah: I have a dear friend named Elizabeth. (Actually, I have two dear friends named Elizabeth, which is very confusing for my other friends, but it is what it is.) Elizabeth and I went to college together and got to know each other as awkward freshmen pledging the same sorority. We fell in love with our husbands at the same time and got married at the same time. Over twenty years later, we vacation together every year. Our kids call each other cousins, and we have been having stimulating conversations about religion and politics and parenting and whatever else is consuming our minds since we first met in that cement block dorm room so long ago.

Elizabeth is a devout Catholic and, upon graduation, was in Kentucky having her first of five children at the same time I was working at Planned Parenthood in North Carolina and telling anyone who would listen I was done with church. In theory, our friendship shouldn't have made it. We lived far apart, including two years when her family lived abroad. We were often in widely divergent phases. She was tackling motherhood for the first time while I was tackling law school. She was moving across the country and figuring out military family life while I was working on Hillary Clinton's presidential campaign in Washington, DC. We have different personalities and different approaches to stress and (probably most confusing to people) we disagree on abortion. And not in some "We'll agree to disagree" way. We both feel so strongly about the issue that agreeing to disagree was never really an option.

When I look back over our first ten years of friendship, especially at the time when we were in very different phases of life, I realize that what kept us together was that passion. I tell people that I fell in love with my husband when I realized I'll always want to know what he thinks about things. I could say the same thing about Elizabeth. Even when I knew she'd disagree with me on things, I was always so interested in how she had gotten there. She's curious and considerate and so, so smart. So, even when we were living very different lives, her way of understanding the world was always interesting to me, because it felt so foreign to how I understood it.

Over time, our lives got less distinct from one another's. Her husband left the military, and they settled in Kentucky. I moved back home to the Bluegrass State myself and started a family. Suddenly we were both in the throes of motherhood, even having babies (her third and my first) months apart. This common language in our lives gave us even more room to explore and grow in our political differences. Through our shared experiences of parenting, we actually moved closer to one another on several issues, including abortion. Within the trusted space of our friendship, we saw that our differences weren't exactly what we'd always imagined. First, we realized that we were trying to find agreement when we were actually talking about different things. She was talking about religion and ethics, and I was talking about politics and policy, especially when I was literally working in that field. Second, once we could distinguish between the two, we felt safe to walk toward each in real ways. Elizabeth will now tell you plainly that outlawing abortion is not a solution to the problem she sees. And I will tell you plainly that our ethics surrounding the value of human life are broken in ways policy can never fix.

We are still different, but we are closer than we have ever been.

....

Once we accept that tension can (and always will) exist in some form between friends, how do we decide when that tension is toxic and the friendship needs to come to an end? We have both had friendships with people we thought would be a part of our lives forever slowly fade or suddenly extinguish in painful ways. No matter if the ending was gradual or sudden, the pain of realizing your friend is gone is real, and it is a grief we find difficult articulating or finding space for in our lives.

Listeners and readers want to know when to walk away from a friendship and when to try to salvage it. Again, we don't have a perfect formula. We know from our own relationship that friction can often just be. It has to occasionally be tended, which can look like a hard conversation, a sacrifice for the other person, or a little break from the other person. But it can just persist in many relationships and form the basis of real growth and depth.

We also know that allowing tension to exist is different from making a friend a *project*. Our friendship works despite our very different personalities, because Sarah isn't trying to make Beth more enthusiastic, and Beth isn't trying to rein Sarah in. When listeners reach out to tell us about friends who won't acknowledge white privilege or believe that the 2020 election was stolen, we're in very different territory. If one person in the relationship decides to stay in the relationship for the sole purpose of changing the other person, that friendship is going to be toxic for both people.

Navigating political tension in friendships requires the same skills that we leaned on in solving our road-trip tension. We have to name what's going on. In friendships stressed by politics, it's really helpful to state the feelings underlying the stress:

- "When you didn't wear a mask, I felt like you were telling me you didn't care about my mother. I understand that wasn't your intention. I also have to be honest about how personally I took it."

- "When I saw who you were voting for in your Instagram story, I felt surprised. It made me wonder what we aren't talking about. I feel like we know each other so well, so I assumed that we were on the same page."
- "When I read your Facebook post, I felt unsettled. It came across in a way that seemed angry and hurtful. I would love to talk about this. I'm not accusing you of anything; I just want to understand what's going on."

We share with audiences all the time that most conversations are happening in two layers. We're discussing a subject, and we're working on our relationship in the process. Long-lasting friends are able to weave in and out of these two subjects in tense political conversations. We can make our points, then say: "Oh, I realize that I'm getting heated talking about this. I'm not mad at you; this is just an area of passion for me." We can also admit that we are mad at each other: "I'm realizing that I'm getting heated here. I'm mad that you feel this way, honestly. I don't like the words you're using to describe other people. I can't believe you support this person. I love you. I want us to stay in this friendship. I'm just mad right now."

Giving voice to this layer of conversation—how our relationship is impacted by the words we're using and the way we're using them—can prevent us from treating our friends like projects. There is a fine line between wanting to influence each other and wanting to manage each other. Checking in with our intentions can help us stay on the healthy side of that line. The two of us frequently remind ourselves and each other that we don't talk politics to convince each other of anything. We talk politics to better understand each other and ourselves. Keeping that curious, growth-oriented posture in our friendships allows them to thrive.

Making the Connection

- Do you have friends that treat you like a project or a problem to be solved? How does that make you feel?
- Do you have friends you worry about constantly? How can you lay down the pressure to fix others?

This is the hardest truth of friendships: many of them are just for a season. Whether it's because the relationship broke over some unsustainable difference of opinion or because life took us in different directions, many people are going to come and go in our lives. Sometimes we grieve that immediately; other times we only recognize it much later.

As we both look back at friendships that have ended—whether by our choice, someone else's choice, or just by time and circumstance—we see a pattern of boundaries being crossed or tensions being buried. It wasn't differences between us and our former friends that ended the relationships. It was how we chose to handle those differences. Sometimes life itself was taking too much from our reserves (like pandemics or divorce or . . . toddlers) to allow us to give anything else to our floundering friendships. Sometimes we realized that the friendships were feeding our own toxic patterns and that it was time to move on.

No matter how the friendship ended, allowing ourselves to grieve *and* to recognize what was gained through the relationships helped us move on and be a better friend to the people still in our lives. When we make a new friend, whether we're four or forty, the thrill of "look at all we share" can help us see each other in a new light. A friendship that illuminates the contours of our differences can be just as exciting. And even if that friendship ends, the insights we've gained remain. Sometimes the insights are painful, and we learn the value of boundaries or the limits of our outreach. Sometimes the insights are exhilarating, and we grow into better and fuller versions of ourselves. Sometimes they're exhilarating and painful all at the same time. That's the power of a good friend.

NOW What?

Spend a minute reflecting on your current and past close friendships. Where you can, express a little gratitude for all you've learned from friendships that are no longer predominant in your life.

For friendships that are predominant in your life now, start a conversation with your nearest and dearest about friendship friction. How have they dealt with it in the past? What's worked? What hasn't? In our experience, people are *hungry* to talk more about healthy friendships, and we're willing to bet your friends aren't any different.

5

Workplaces

From the Food Chain to the Garden

Beth: In September 2006, I arrived at a downtown Cincinnati office tower for my first day of work as a lawyer. I can feel the sensation of walking through the elevator lobby like it was yesterday. There were bodies all around me—bodies dressed in well-tailored suits, bodies carrying leather briefcases and avoiding eye contact, and bodies scrolling BlackBerrys (remember those?). It felt like a sea of bodies, not a sea of people.

I grew up in a rural area (population 1,500 with two banks, one grocery store, and zero stoplights) where we waved to strangers in cars and said "Hello" and "How are the kids?" reflexively to passersby. There was a distinct person-ness to every human I encountered. I don't mean to romanticize it. My hometown earned its share of small-town stereotypes. There was gossip and exclusivity and conformity and general nosiness. But there was also a sense that every person was a whole person with a family, a history, friendships, and a full universe of thoughts and feelings.

In the elevator lobby of that law firm, I couldn't feel that whole person-ness in the bodies around me, and that affected my very cells. I remember pressing the button for the eighteenth floor and seeing myself standing there in my not-well-tailored suit, as though I was looking down from the moon. There was the darkness of the universe, the swirl of oceans and clouds, a country, a city, an office building, and a girl who did not belong in it. I walked out of the elevator a bit dizzy. Despite lots of genuine friendships and learning that developed over time, I'm not sure that dizziness left me until my last day with the firm eleven years later.

Like so many people, I found myself in a job that I could do reasonably well but that I could not quite embody. The excellent salary and benefits, the professional environment, the impressive business card—none of it filled the hole of wanting to belong in my space with my coworkers. Almost nothing was really wrong, but I spent extra minutes in the parking garage every morning, willing myself to actually go into the office. I spent extra minutes in the parking garage every evening, wiping away tears and composing myself enough for the commute home.

....

Most Americans will spend a full third of their lives (roughly ninety thousand hours) working. Pre-pandemic, 78 percent of workers who logged thirty to fifty working hours weekly spent more time with their colleagues than with their families.[1] The pandemic certainly altered that balance of raw hours for many of us, but the push to carry on has meant more time stuck to the screen. If the workplace changes accelerated by the pandemic become permanent, then even more Zoom meetings are not going to alleviate the loneliness Beth felt on her first day or the artificial barrier many of us feel between ourselves and our colleagues.

Whole person-ness is essential to sustainable work. This doesn't mean we have to love our coworkers like family. (Sometimes that metaphor is used to justify some truly unacceptable workplace behavior.) It simply means we have to be able to show up at work as ourselves. When we're hiding essential aspects of who we are, we are susceptible to carrying a pervasive sense of scarcity around work—fearing that we aren't enough, fearing that we'll lose out, fearing that any conflict will leave us on the outside looking in.

Whether you're a person who looks to work for a sense of identity and reward or a person who "works to live, not the other way around," we think it's important to find a work environment where you can be yourself. After all, we practice power dynamics at work. Our attitudes about authority are shaped on some level by workplace policies. Our attitudes about leadership are shaped on some level by supervisors and executives. Our attitudes about how much we can trust other people are shaped on some level by our colleagues. If we work in an environment where we can't be ourselves, we internalize a sense that power robs us of who we are and that we can't do much about that.

This is especially true now that politics has gone from an avoided topic at work to an unavoidable piece of every organization. From small businesses who had to battle customers over masks to giant corporations who took stands on systemic racism, national politics now affects so many parts of our work, making already delicate (sometimes strained) relationships even worse.

Work is a microcosm for the rest of society, and our experiences at work profoundly influence our values when it comes to politics. The experiences we've had with labor unions and the positions we occupy vis-à-vis those unions will inform our support or opposition to collective bargaining and right-to-work laws. Sarah's stepfather had a bad experience with labor unions in the seventies and still won't hear a word about the good they do in the labor market. If your business relied on lumber during the spring of 2021, you are going to carry ideas about trade policy far longer than the rest of us who stopped paying attention once our toilet paper showed up. This interplay between individual work experiences and broader policy is central to our democracy. We want those work experiences and the values they represent to show up in politics prominently. It is how a citizen-government thrives.

So, we must acknowledge our workplace feelings and look for environments where we can flourish.

Finding Our Places

Beth: When I was in law school, the dean of career services assembled all of us in the mock courtroom to prepare for summer job interviews. It was 2004, and we were beginning to learn about the law firm economy at the time. Basically, it went like this: Get really good grades your first semester of law school so you can get a really good summer job, which will lead to a really good second summer job, which will lead to a good job offer your third year. Tank in the first semester, and best of luck to you! (There were notable exceptions to this pattern but not many.)

The dean was a kind, caring person, and she was refreshingly honest. I will never, as long as I live, forget her talk that day. She told us she was going to be straight with us about law firm culture. We would be interviewed by mostly men. They were going to prefer women who wore skirts to women who wore pants. They were going to prefer white button-down shirts and dark jackets. They were going to prefer very conventional hairstyles. She told us to cover any tattoos and remove any piercings other than one hole in each ear for women only. "I know some of you are thinking, *but I'm an individual!*" she said, quietly, as though she truly hated having to level with us. "Please recognize that being an individual will result in unemployment."

Wanting to feel appreciated as individual in all aspects of our lives is normal and healthy. And yet showing up as our whole selves is fraught when money and promotions and power are *on the line.* Workplace hierarchy (understood through organizational charts, titles, and salaries) and workplace politics (understood through only slightly subtler cues like lunch invitations, workspace placements, and the quality of assignments) keep everyone slightly off-balance. There is an undercurrent of scarcity: you can always mess up in exactly the wrong way, and if you do, someone will be happy to replace you.

That style of management has obviously failed us, and many workplaces are recognizing it. We tend to use lots of animal kingdom metaphors in the workplace: talking about where people are on the food chain, saying that it's a dog-eat-dog world, looking for the alpha, etc. We prefer to go plant-based. Workplaces are like gardens, with different kinds of plants trying to grow together to bear fruit. Leadership exists to tend to those plants—figuring out how and where to grow them, caring for them, considering sunshine, climate, and soil—in order to create the desired harvest. We're encouraged by conversations about servant leadership, trusting employees to work remotely, healthy unionization campaigns, and other movements in workplaces to provide workers with greater autonomy, power, and respect.

Even the best leadership doesn't make every environment suitable for us. Amazing plants require very particular climates to flourish. It took years for Beth to understand that the out-of-body feeling she described at the beginning of this chapter did not signal that she was in a bad place. It also didn't signal that she was inadequate for that work. It simply wasn't a match. She was in the wrong ecosystem.

Bringing this sensibility—that our environments need to be right for who we are and where we are in our careers—removes some of the fear and scarcity that can accompany work. It frees us of harsh judgments that we tend to make about ourselves and our colleagues. It invites us to see our own needs and the needs of others.

Making the Connection

- Imagine yourself in your workplace garden. Are you planted well? Are you receiving the sunlight and water you need?
- What would flourishing at work mean for you?

Developing Our Courage

Sarah: My very first job out of college was at Planned Parenthood, and my boss, Karen, was amazing. We had weekly lunches where she would ask me how I was doing and help me navigate any challenges. When I did a particularly good job, she brought me little gifts from Aveda and local boutiques! My next boss, Hal, was equally supportive (although there were no presents, an issue I pointed out over and over again, much to Hal's chagrin). He always allowed me to learn and take on new challenges and made me feel smart and valued. Hal and I are still friends to this day (and there are still no presents!).

And yet, I will tell anyone who asks that I can't have a boss. It took me two decades and my husband saying plainly one day, "You don't like having a boss. That's OK," to figure that out. I had internalized the idea that wanting the freedom of working with a partner or for myself was a character flaw. It's not that a boss represents cruelty or abuse to me; it's that having a boss (even a great one) represents a loss of freedom. I'd absorbed the message that good work was scarce and that having a good boss was the best I deserved. In a way, my great bosses helped me undo that message. By making me feel seen and appreciated beyond my work, they taught me that I was more than the job I did.

By being great bosses, they'd given me the strength to go out and be my own.

....

Dominant cultural messages are filled with pressure and contradictory expectations surrounding work and the values it is supposed to represent. There is a definitive cultural message that college education is the path to economic prosperity, yet economic prosperity is hard to experience when student loan debt defines so many household budgets. There is a definitive cultural message that we should love what we do and also that we should be grateful for any job that we get. We're told to make as much money as possible but also to take unpaid internships in order to get there. We're told not to get too close to our coworkers but also to crave our boss's approval. We're told not to find our identities through work but "What do you do?" is the first question we ask one another. We're told to give work our all for decades and then asked to leave organizations at the drop of a hat without looking back.

We are told to be successful, and all of us want to be successful. We just need broader definitions of success. Right now, we understand success to mean growth and growth to mean accumulation. If the only way to be successful is to make more and more and more money, while amassing more and more and more power, it's no wonder that we're, as author Anne Helen Petersen describes in *Can't Even: How Millennials Became the Burnout Generation*, in a constant state of precarity. Those feelings of precarity and scarcity both at work and about work aren't values, they are fears. Using fear as a driver is always dangerous, but it is particularly problematic when politics comes into play.

Defining success for yourself is an act of courage. Your definition might be something like "aligning my values with the way that I spend my time." It might be about conscientiousness or care. You might find, as we do, that you value autonomy. Perhaps work for you is about creating greater justice. All these forms of success can exist in any job, as long as you're in an environment where you can grow and as long as you trust yourself to discern whether you're in the right place for you. Our experience has been that people who've courageously defined success on their own terms see that courage multiply. They show up fully for projects, meetings, and colleagues. They do not shy away from sharing their opinions, and they stay grounded when things get tough.

Finding our courage at work is critical to the exercise of our political power. If we can share our thoughts on the company's new remote-work policy clearly and openly, we can step into political activism. If we can look at a coworker who's not working out and say, "This must not be the right environment for you," we can tap into greater empathy in the political sphere. If we can engage in healthy conflict with our coworkers, we can do the same with our fellow citizens. The stakes at work always feel very high for good reasons—money, livelihood, and our daily operations are on the line. All of this makes work the perfect place to develop ourselves as strong, assertive people who look out for ourselves while caring for those around us.

Making the Connection

- What does success mean to you?
- How does that definition of success align with your current job?
- Where do you find courage at work? Where might you show even greater courage?

Lead with Your Values

Sarah: As with so many areas of life, the traditional approach to work for so many people is to keep their heads down and keep politics out of it. Of course, that approach is increasingly difficult in our current polarized environment, but as someone who has worked in politics for most of her adult life, it was never really an option.

I've worked at the National Organization for Women and Planned Parenthood, where my bosses and I shared our personal journeys with feminism and reproductive rights. I've worked for members of Congress and spent lunch breaks debating Medicare and immigration policy with fellow staffers. I've worked for campaigns and spent long nights sharing my passion for changing the world with coworkers just as devoted as I was. There is a particular joy in working in a space where deep conversations on the political issues of our time are not only present but welcome.

And yet, power dynamics are on full display in the halls of power. Issues of scarcity are definitely present, especially in the tiny world of congressional staffing and campaign work. In a way, conflicts over political issues are particularly devastating inside the insular world of political work. During my time on Hillary Clinton's campaign in 2007, I was frustrated and hurt by the constant sexist chatter of some of my coworkers. One coworker, in particular, would remark on the appearance of female reporters and what he perceived to be the overall deficiencies of women in media. When I confronted him over his sexist comments, he replied, "I can't be sexist. I work for Hillary Clinton."

I knew he was wrong and told him so, but I also knew that expressing my discomfort to anyone but him wasn't likely to help me move up the ranks of the campaign. That my coworkers and I shared politics didn't absolve us of tension and strain inside our workplace. The fear that being fully who we were would lead to less was ever present—less pay, less opportunity, less promotion. In a way, the conflicts about identity were even harder in space built around what we all perceived as shared values.

....

Political expression within a workplace can lead to meaningful shifts in power. When workers organize, collective bargaining usually leads to improved pay and working conditions. Prior to the Supreme Court's landmark decision in *Obergefell v. Hodges* (making marriages among two people of the same sex legal throughout the United States), workers advocated for companies to recognize their colleagues' relationships. Affinity groups within workplaces advocate for fairer, more inclusive environments. Women's groups have effectively advocated for more generous family leave policies than required by the Family and Medical Leave Act and for programs to support new mothers upon their return to work after giving birth.

Workers, especially those from the millennial generation, pressure employers to be more politically active because they want to work at places that reflect their values.[2] In 2020, over two hundred fifty employees at Microsoft signed a letter advocating for the company to end its work with law enforcement entities and support criminal justice reforms in its home city of Seattle.

Gen Z workers are also demanding that their companies explicitly advocate for initiatives to advance racial equity, to combat climate change, and to advance LGBTQ+ equality. Corporations are giving unprecedented amounts of money to programs that support education and investment in communities of color.

The flip side of this political advocacy within companies is the concern—sometimes real and sometimes imagined—about cancel culture. These conversations are inextricably tied up with conversations around the #MeToo movement. For some, watching powerful men stripped of their power after decades of abuse was the fullest manifestation of their values at the workplace and, beyond #MeToo, showed us that in some workplaces, differences in power dynamics led to cruelty, harassment, or abuse. Many of the people engaged in toxic behavior were propped up by others within their workplaces for a variety of reasons: because they made the company a lot of money, because they amassed powerful friends, because their conduct gave cover to the conduct of others. Whatever the reasons, in too many workplaces, completely unacceptable behavior was not only accepted but rewarded. This problem is as old as work itself and is far from over.

Social media and other factors are lowering our societal tolerance for unacceptable behavior, and we believe this is a long overdue good. It is important for companies to establish and enforce clear expectations, even and especially for those who occupy positions of power.

However, for others, watching the societal understanding of power change dramatically in a short period of time led to a lot of fear and anxiety. Because people are people, our efforts toward heightened standards of conduct and attempts at greater accountability are imperfect. There are times when we leap to conclusions without first investigating all the facts. We impose punishments that do not fit the crimes. Sometimes that's a lost job. Sometimes that's an opportunity withheld. Sometimes that's a barrage of social media harassment that leads to threats and violence. With so many "cancelations" playing out very publicly, many of us started to internalize a fear: "If I show up as my full self at work, someone might not like it, and because they might not like it, I might lose out."

— *Making the Connection* —————

- Where do you see fear at your workplace?
- Do you feel fearful that saying or doing something that feels right to you will lead to negative ramifications at your workplace? Are there conversations at your workplace around cancel culture? Are your co-workers expressing fear that they might get canceled?

In many ways, those fears are well placed. We have not yet figured out how to hold responsibility and redemption together. (Look no further than our criminal legal system to see that in the context of literal crime and deprivation of actual liberty.) And also—this fear is not helping anyone. We are going to have to build our muscles over time—the muscles that help us stand up to toxic behavior and the muscles that help us know when it's time to forgive and move on.

We are going to have to learn to acknowledge fear without condoning it or giving in. Sarah has always loved the way author Elizabeth Gilbert described her process in her book *Big Magic: Creative Living beyond Fear.* She tells anxiety and fear they're going on a road trip. She understands they are needed and can't be left behind entirely. However, they cannot be allowed to drive or sit in the front seat. Fear and anxiety are allowed in the car, but they have to sit in the back.

> **Focusing conversations on values, while still acknowledging one another's fears, will have to start somewhere and sometimes that is with our own individual understanding.**

We realize a cute metaphor isn't the secret to our workplace tension surrounding politics or anything else. However, focusing conversations on values, while still acknowledging one another's fears, will have to start somewhere and sometimes that is with our own individual understanding. That's finding your courage. If you are a leader at your workplace, then obviously you are in an even better position to influence these conversations. If you feel powerless at your workplace, then perhaps the goal isn't to influence the entire workplace culture but to influence one other coworker by acknowledging their fears and affirming their values.

Your goal also might be simply developing your capacity to lead with your values. There are opportunities to do this every day at work:

- Develop a practice of sharing any kind words you say or hear about a colleague with them directly. People love to receive a quick text or email saying, "Hey, are your ears burning? A customer was just raving about your presentation from last week!" or "Just wanted to let you know that I met with the CEO and shared that you were indispensable on our project!"

- Try to respect others' time in everything that you do. A very simple starting point is crafting specific subject lines for emails that indicate whether a response is needed and, if so, how soon.

- Use your voice in situations where conflict will arise. Tensions can fester in Slack, email chains, and texts. If there's a problem, use your voice to announce it and work through it. (Don't worry, phone-haters! You can record a voice memo and email it, if that's your preference.) We like to follow a simple formula in addressing conflict: "This is going to be a tough conversation about vacation time, but we wanted to share a problem that we're finding. We're talking about this with you because we care about this relationship and want it to work well, especially regarding how we take time off to care for ourselves. Here's what we're noticing: [insert positive content]."

- Object to objectionable behaviors. You don't have to know what to say in the moment that something goes wrong. Take your time, and plan what you want to share in three bullet points or less. If you saw someone treated unfairly, say so. If you believe a new policy marginalizes someone, say so. If an issue was handled badly, say so. Leading with your values means that you speak up to the appropriate leader (not to everyone in the workplace—that's just gossip), with the good intention of making the workplace better.

We can lead with our values and find that we're rewarded in unexpected ways. If you're in an environment where you can flourish, you'll find that grace-filled truth telling is rewarded with trust, admiration, and likely, greater responsibility. If you're not, you'll probably experience some difficult moments.

And just like in our families and with our friends, sometimes we have to walk away. Even in the face of financial precarity, there are times when a workplace becomes unsustainable for us. We love the natural world for giving us yet another metaphor appropriate to the workplace: *seasons.* You will find there are times when, perhaps inexplicably, you need to shift. Whether you're beginning a new season, wrapping one up, or growing through one, we wish for you a workplace environment where you find courage that extends far beyond the place that pays your bills.

NOW What?

- Have you ever left a job? What motivated you to leave? How did you push past the fear?
- What are the values motivating you at your workplace? Where do you see those values reflected in your workplace as a whole?
- Are there places you feel like your values could be better reflected at your workplace? What might you need to lead with your values?

Part Two

THOSE FARTHER AWAY

We spent the first half of this book trying to dig beneath political conflict to find hidden expectations, hidden fears, even hidden expertise. We hope you already see that the lessons we learn in our personal relationships can also apply outside those relationships. Fears are driving conflict at home as well as at work. Personality differences can put tension in a marriage as well as a friendship. As we learn to see one connection more clearly, we learn to see all connections more clearly, and now the real work begins. We want to spend the second half of the book talking about those we are connected to whom we don't see every day (or ever in our lives!). We want to examine the connection to the fellow congregants we might only see once a week or the fellow public school parents we might only see once a year at the fall carnival. We want to examine the connection to the government employee who manages your water flow or the fellow citizen whose heart is breaking on your local news broadcast. We want to examine the connection to every single human being we share this planet with because that connection matters, and the lessons we learn from those we break bread with every day can be applied to those with whom we might never share a table.

6

Community—Churches and Nonprofits and Schools

Why Churches Don't Belong on Yelp

Sarah: I stopped attending church for ten years. I was raised Southern Baptist and spent most every Sunday and Wednesday of my childhood sitting in the pews, singing in the choir, or hanging with the youth group. It is easier with the gift of many decades to see what was gained during that time. I felt supported and loved. I felt like people were rooting for me. I also learned values that have stuck with me my entire life—forgiveness, charity, compassion.

But I stopped attending for so long because faith, hope, and love were not the only things I learned. I learned I was not good enough and that there were rules about who was on the inside and who was on the outside. So, for most of my twenties, I proudly claimed my place on the outside. If you'd have asked me,

I would have told you the church was fundamentally broken, and I didn't want to participate in propping up a broken institution.

Then I became a mom. Suddenly, everything I had so neatly sorted out for myself didn't seem fair to decide on behalf of my kids. I would find myself tearing up every time Lee Ann Womack sang, "Promise me you'll give faith a fighting chance."[1] (Perhaps my devotion to country music extends beyond the 1990s.) I wanted my boys to give faith a fighting chance. Just because my faith had taken a beating didn't mean they shouldn't get a shot in the ring.

So, we started attending our local Episcopal church. (My husband had been raised Episcopal and pointed out that he didn't carry the same baggage I did.) At first, I was doing it for our boys. I never expected that three years later I would be standing in front of my family being confirmed into a faith I thought I had left behind. Faith that still very much exists in the presence of questions and doubts. Based on my past, I think deep down I expected to be found out and expelled for those doubts. I grew up believing it was all or nothing. Believe. Fall in line. Or get out.

But in our church, literally called Grace, there is room for my questions. In fact, it seems everyone has them. There is grace for our different journeys. There is grace for the institution itself and everyone in it. When our rector gives a sermon I disagree with, I think, *Well, there will be another one next week.* When one of my beloved church ladies gets a little too bossy, I just smile and get the heck out of her way. Sometimes our family is all in on church, and sometimes the seasons of life pull us in another direction so we are the ones asking for grace.

I've now been back in church for as long as I was absent, and it is that flow of grace that most steadily defines my relationship to church. Long gone is the obsession with rules and judgment (not all the way gone—I am an Enneagram 1, after all). I no longer think about institutions as failing because any institution composed of human beings is both succeeding and failing all at the same time. And I try to remember that as a human being in that institution I will sometimes succeed at bringing faith, hope, and love to my people. Sometimes I will fail, and I will also need grace when I do.

....

Lee Ann Womack's "I Hope You Dance" might have inspired Sarah to return to church, but since the song was released over twenty years ago (ouch), church attendance among Americans has declined by almost 20 percent, according to Gallup.[2] This dramatic drop tracks alongside a doubling of Americans who report no religious affiliation. And it's not just those with no affiliation who account for the drop in church attendance; those who grew up with a strong religious affiliation are abandoning or deconstructing their faiths as well. This decline in church membership tracks with a decline in other civic participation. Membership in organizations like Rotary Clubs, Lions' Clubs, and Kiwanis has been plummeting for decades. Even organizations that serve kids and families, like Scouts and YMCA, are projecting tough financial futures amid decreasing membership. COVID-19 closed some of our favorite neighborhood hangouts, and it's unclear how and where we'll gather in our communities post-pandemic.

There are reasons that community and religious institutions are struggling. Many organizations have been built on exclusive foundations. Too many have perpetuated racism, discrimination against LGBTQ+ people, and marginalization of women. There have been abuses of power, scandals, and financial crimes. There have been selfish leaders and followers who lacked the courage and fortitude to challenge those leaders. Those organizations deserve to struggle and even fail.

The realization that brought both of us back to church after a period of absence is this: there is not one church. And this realization has connected us more deeply to numerous organizations in our communities.

We talk about our institutions—be it church or school or charity organizations—as if they are one thing. Church can include everything from Saddleback to a small group of people gathering in one another's homes. Public schools can include everything from public charter schools in Manhattan to one-room schoolhouses in Montana. Nonprofits can include everything from Planned Parenthood to a local soup kitchen. Our institutions are tiny and large, formal and informal, thriving and failing.

The diversity of our institutions reflects the diversity of the people who compose them. And that is what gets lost in conversations about our institutions—they are simply organizations of people. Institutions aren't one thing because they aren't a thing at all. Church isn't religion. Church is how we come together as a group to practice our faith. School isn't education. School is how we come together to educate our children. Nonprofits aren't charity. Nonprofits are how we come together to help one another. These institutions are simply people coming together for a common purpose.

In so many ways and in so many institutions, we've lost sight of that purpose because we've started treating our institutions like products.

Participation Not Consumption

Consumption is a fundamental part of American life. Capitalism is our primary economic system, and capitalism is built around consumption. From the moment we are born, we are trained up as consumers. The average American sees between six thousand to ten thousand advertisements every single day.[3] All those messages teach us one thing: Every problem we have (whether created by the ad itself or truly felt inside our lives) can be solved by purchasing.

Look, we will be the first to admit that sometimes that's true! Sarah's heated mattress pad has solved a lifelong struggle of trying to fall asleep with ice cold feet (and don't get her started on her Peloton . . . No seriously, please don't get her started). Beth will talk to you all day about cooking gadgets. (How did we live without Instant Pots and Air Fryers?) We all have beloved products that have changed our lives. Sometimes consumption solves problems. It's just that consumption doesn't solve every kind of problem, and it's not the only or best kind of solution available to us.

We've been taught that consumption fixes everything, which has fundamentally limited our creativity. More insidiously, we've learned from this relentless marketing to act like consumers no matter the context.

Seeing thousands of messages directed to us only through our identity as consumers bolsters that identity. We inhabit it, however subconsciously, when we see an ad or research a product or make a decision to purchase. We act as a consumer hundreds of times a day when we decide where or what to eat, what to wear, where to shop, what to buy. Even as we do a better job considering the impact of buying on the planet, our decision-making as consumers remains highly individualized: Do I have enough money to buy this? Will this fill my belly or make me look cute or make my kids happy?

It's not wrong to be a consumer. In the economic context, it serves us to keep our needs front and center. We've built a thriving economy through a consumer mentality. We've built some amazing and life-giving products. Consumption becomes a problem when we bring that mentality everywhere, especially to institutions that are asking us to be so much more.

If institutions are formed to serve a common purpose, what happens when we each show up with only our individual needs in mind?

Making the Connection

We've all been guilty of acting like a disgruntled consumer inside our institutions. Let's go ahead and exorcise those demons now. Give a good old-fashioned Yelp review to your church/your school/your organization. Write down your gripes and your frustrations and go all in on that ugly lobby decor that sets your hair on fire.

Now pull an Abe Lincoln, who was famous for writing letters and throwing them away, and put that review in the trash. See if you feel any better.

The Customer Isn't Always Right (Especially When They're Not a Customer)

When we reduce the institution to a product, we see it as distinct and different from ourselves and our participation in it. We aren't a part of the lay ministry of the church; we are audience members in front of a stage. We aren't citizen members of the local school district; we are disgruntled taxpayers who believe we aren't getting our money's worth. We aren't supporters of a local charitable cause; we are donors with a list of our own priorities. We're not joining the institution. We're reviewing—giving it four stars on Yelp and then moving on. The institution becomes a hero or, more likely, a villain (because everybody is the Brothers Grimm on Yelp, let us tell you!) when the whole time the institution is *us*. And we rarely pause to assess the reasonableness of our views. Our commercial culture tells us that the customer is always right.

Every piece of that mantra damages our institutions (and even our businesses as we've learned during the pandemic). We expect teachers and ministers to educate, comfort, and lead . . . and also respond to our emails with the efficiency of a customer service center. Even when we're volunteering our time, we expect to have a four-star experience. Being a customer is not a commitment. If you don't like what's happening, you take your business elsewhere. In any community of people, things will happen that we don't like. The beauty of organizations organized around common purposes is in the commitment to stick around anyway. Sticking around anyway helps us grow. It gives us the chance to see what happens when someone else has a better idea, to contribute to a vision we disagreed with, to realize the fruits of messy labor.

The "customer is always right" mentality gets worse when we are also giving financially to our institutions. It is unsurprising that our training as consumers surfaces when we are giving actual money to many of our local institutions. We tithe to our local church so shouldn't we have a say in how the money is spent? We pay taxes for the local school so shouldn't we be able to complain about the state of education? We give donations to our local nonprofits so shouldn't we make sure they're spending our money on helping people instead of overhead? (PSA: Overhead is important in every organization, whether it's for-profit or nonprofit. Venture capitalists have really messed up our mindset around this.)

When we come together as a group to achieve a common goal, everybody cannot be right all the time—even if they are major donors (ask someone who fundraises for a living!). Those of us with young children in our lives learned that lesson the hard way when it came to public school during the pandemic. Participating in institutions, much like healthy partnerships and parenting and friendship, requires a release of the need and desire to control everything. Institutions ask us for gifts, not investments—gifts in the form of time, talent, money, and emotional energy. Most of the time, we will end up getting something back from the institution. That "return" is made more precious by the fact that we don't get to choose what it is or how and when it comes to us.

The limitations of the consumer mindset can be seen prominently in public schools, which have a never-ending list of constituents: students, parents, volunteers, teachers, administrators, taxpayers, politicians. Teachers have endless examples of parents who act like the teacher works for them instead of with them educating their child. Board members have sat through meetings where taxpayers come and complain about costs (or worse, politics) at local meetings. Volunteers know what it's like to be invisible to school administrators. And when all these different constituents believe they are right, the situation can become untenable.

We both come from families filled with schoolteachers. We've been raised with the understanding that too many people believe they are educational experts simply because they attended school and the knowledge that *actual* educational experts are rarely afforded the respect they deserve. We admit to falling into the I-know-better-than-the-school trap ourselves, as evidenced by many, many text messages between us about school disciplinary practices that seem dated and, we confess, asinine to us. (We're looking at you, clip stick!) COVID-19 gave all of us a miserable opportunity to reexamine our relationships with schools. Suddenly, we couldn't act like customers because we were the ones running the store! In our households, the time our kids spent in "virtual school" opened our eyes to new information about our kids, their schools, and ourselves.

Beth: I'm going to come clean about my arrogance going into virtual schooling. I wanted to crush it. I wanted the kids in my immediate circle to walk out of the school year feeling like it was the best ever because Mom is The World's Best At-Home Teacher.™ Maybe a part of me had always been homeschool-curious. The ability to influence and broaden what the kids thought about every day, to allow them to explore some of their interests in deeper ways sparked a little creativity in me.

I also did not want to face the challenge alone. Three other families in my neighborhood were taking COVID-19 precautions that mirrored our family's and also seemed to approach school with a similar mindset to ours. I liked and trusted the parents and kids in those families and proposed that we work together as a pod. We made a plan, a schedule, and got to it. Our kids packed their backpacks every day, rotated houses, and had lesson plans for when their class calls ended.

It lasted a few weeks.

I loved aspects of those weeks. In some ways, they met and exceeded my expectations about how wonderful it could be to take a more active role in our kids' education. It ended because our plan was in dramatic tension with the school's plan. Teachers managing classrooms of fifteen to thirty kids were planning days that required each kid to be in a quiet space with a screen. The lively, colorful rooms we set up in our homes were too loud and distracting for the myriad Google Meets the kids were required to attend. It felt like we were competing with the school, and the school had to win.

As our school struggled to figure out how to bring kids back into classrooms—two days a week, now four, now two again, now just in the morning, now four until next week then five, maybe, hopefully—I wished often that I had just pulled my kids out of public school for the year. It was especially painful that the long days at home, in quiet spaces with a screen, involved so much complaining. "I just want to go back to school!" "I miss my friends!" "This call is sooooo boring!" Then, when they finally were able to be back in their classrooms to wrap the 2020–2021 school year, they complained. "I hate wearing masks at school!" "I wish I could just stay here!" "My class is sooooo boring!"

Several truths exist at one time. The school did the best it could, and its best was fine. I could have done a better job for my daughters on our own. There was still value in keeping them connected with their peers, teachers, and administrators. They didn't learn as much as they could have. They still learned. They are fine. They are scarred. They are better off than so many kids in different circumstances. They will still be dealing with the consequences of this year for a long time.

Sarah: I vividly remember telling Beth when Japan announced it would shut down school for a MONTH in March of 2020. We both assured each other that such a massive shutdown (or so it seemed at the time) was definitely out of an abundance of caution surrounding the Olympics, and that would never happen in the United States. A month without our kids in school seemed impossible. I had one relationship with the public school system—complete and total dependence.

I grew up around educators. My mother was a high school librarian. My grandmother was a guidance counselor. My great-grandmother taught business at the local community college. I grew up listening to long conversations about the complicated ecosystem of state regulators, school boards, administrators, parents, teachers, and students. I understood that from the moment my first son started kindergarten I was a small cog in a very big machine. As a result, I'd say my approach as a parent was very hands-off. I've gone to the school to complain only once in a decade. I've never challenged a grade my child received. I've even skipped parent-teacher conferences.

Of course, hands-off wasn't really an option for most of 2020. Suddenly, the shutdown in Japan looked less like an outlier and more like a harbinger of things to come. When remote learning began, I was spending hours on curriculum plans that would keep my kids busy for a total of forty-five minutes. As it dragged on, I was struggling to keep my kids on track across apps and grade levels and varying levels of interest. Hands-off simply wasn't an option, and it was only thanks to our village, including family and paid help, that we made it through.

As with most hard things, I learned a lot. I learned my dependence on the public school system was well placed. My kids need school, and I need my kids in school for a million different reasons I wouldn't have been able to articulate in 2019. Their presence in the school system goes so far beyond learning and socialization. I also saw that my hands-off approach has its limits and that I have an active role to play in helping my boys navigate an institution I have a tendency to take for granted. Not because I'm trying to rig the system in their favor but because the system works best when I'm helping them do their best within it. My oldest son needed to learn study skills and organization. My middle son was able to go off his ADHD medication during quarantine and is now succeeding at school without it. My youngest son started kindergarten in the fall of 2020 and has probably had the hardest time with the on-again-off-again virtual school. I learned that sometimes the best role I can play as a parent is being a soft place to land after struggles at school.

I didn't just learn how to support them, I learned how to support my friends who are teachers and other parents struggling within the system. I also learned that the entire institution needs an enormous amount of care, far beyond 2020. COVID exposed so many issues and problems within our public school systems while also showing us all how deeply we need the institution itself. Hands-off no longer seems like the best option for me. Not because I don't trust the school, but because I care too much about its future.

....

Whether we love a kid or a teacher, are employed by a school, study education, or pay taxes, we participate in and influence our schools. At some point in our participation, we'll encounter something that we adamantly disagree with or perceive as unfair and unjust. We will , on occasion, have a point, at least as to *our* kid, *this* teacher, or this *one* topic that we understand well. Something could always be better. Resources could always be allocated differently. More perspectives could always be included.

But we're not comparison shopping. We're not hunting the best deals for our tax dollars. When we participate instead of consume, the fact that something could be better is an invitation—not a deal breaker.

None of this is to say that institutions are perfect. Many institutions have highly complex and hierarchical structures of power that work hard to exclude the people who compose the majority of the institution. Most institutions will go off course at some point. (They're just collections of human beings! It's inevitable!) And there are few if any institutions where we can come in as individuals and change the whole thing.

That's the glorious point—we don't have to! Consumerism teaches us to think of our presence in any place as transactional. It teaches us the only role we have to play is as individuals making individual decisions. I give you my time/energy/presence, and you give me spiritual guidance/an education/a way to help. But that's not how it works (or even should work) inside our community institutions.

Change Isn't Judgment

The other problem with approaching our institutions as consumers is it doesn't equip us to adjust to new circumstances. Consumerism gives us one tool for adapting to change: take it or leave it. No matter your age, we've all listened to the adults in our lives complain about the "trashy new styles" of clothes that expose too much skin or the "noisy annoying" new style of music that gets on their nerves. The solution before them is always simple—change the station, shop at the store that makes you feel comfortable, use your dollars to voice your criticism. (Side note: it is alarming to wake up one day and see your peers rehashing these lines that your parents' generation rolled out in the face of change.) We understand nostalgia, but something else seems to be going on when otherwise sensible people lose their cool over change.

Remember when we talked about overidentifying with our emotions in chapter 2? We suspect that's our culprit in local institutions too. Our emotions show up to tell us seriously unhelpful things about changes as judgments of our past experiences and criticisms of who we are. New math must be garbage because the way we learned it was just fine, thank you very much. The new executive director can't possibly be as good as the old one. Changing our religious doctrines must be an abandonment of our values instead of a shift in our understanding. If something is changing and we didn't choose the change, it must reflect poorly on us. It must mean that we're being rejected. And, if you don't accept us and all our preferences, then we can just leave the congregation/school district/organization.

We all know deep down that change is not a rejection of our previous individual decisions—just like we all know (deep down) the genius of Jay-Z isn't a rejection of the genius of The Beatles. Knowing and feeling are sadly different. We're not here to dole out shame for having emotional responses to change. We're here to see and affirm your emotions and ask you to gently consider whether they tell the entirety of the story. We also want to acknowledge that not all change is improvement. Some changes, especially in churches, schools, and nonprofits, come about because they are objectively better. Some are better for the moment. Some make a situation worse. When that happens, we learn from it and try again. We have to remember that there can be no innovation without failure.

And many changes are just different. Not better. Not worse. Just different. We talked about the need of adult children to grow into beliefs and lifestyles that differ from their families of origin. Institutions are composed of people who embody that need to create. It is fundamental to who we are. We want to leave our marks, and so we do. There is so much peace in embracing that creativity and using our voices to contribute as we can.

Institutions are suffering because, in the face of change, so many people are rejecting the institution outright and making the room smaller. They are suffering because we keep making their rooms smaller, which makes those rooms more suffocating. Some important questions are staring at those of us who are tightly connected to these institutions. How do we make our rooms bigger and release pressure inside of them? How do we meet present needs and preserve the best of our past traditions? How do we let go of the forces that incubate abuse, trauma, neglect, and oppression? How do we make amends for the harm we've done? How do we share and increase the good that we do?

And for those of us who have left, how do we find a new place to participate and contribute? We truly believe that somewhere in the landscape of every community, there is an institution in which everyone can contribute authentically and meaningfully. Our participation might always be seasonal: times to enter and times to leave, times in the wilderness and times in the village. But our participation, in its seasons and for purposes that feel noble to us, is essential for both us and our communities.

Because our participation (not our pocketbooks) is where the real power lies.

Making the Connection

Consider an organization that you're a part of or that you've been a part of in the past. Are there places where you've approached it with a consumer mindset? How has that impacted your relationship with the institution? How do you think it might have impacted others within the institution?

Showing Up as a Contributor

We're asking you to spot and drop the consumer mindset about institutions. Now what?

We can see our presence as part of the whole. We are threads woven in the fabric of connection—threads that will sometimes ravel or break but that can always be tied together again.

Perhaps we might shift our orientation from customer or even member (which has taken on a lot of different connotations, most of which keep us in a transactional mindset) to contributor. What might it mean to consider that we have something to offer institutions, and that our offering is our purpose in showing up? We join the board because we have a skill that the board needs. We stay in the church despite some doctrinal differences because our perspective matters. We contribute to the public school because we are community members who can represent certain aspects of community needs and opportunities.

> We are threads woven in the fabric of connection—threads that will sometimes ravel or break but that can always be tied together again.

We can act as contributors even when we are primarily recipients of the services of one of these institutions. Beth's church has a shower ministry for people experiencing homelessness. At designated hours, people from the community may show up to use the church's showers, no questions asked. They receive basic toiletries, a fresh pair of socks, a hot beverage, and a kind interaction with the church staff and volunteers. The people taking the showers are contributing to that ministry with every interaction, even as they receive its benefits. They help the church understand the scope of needs in the community. They share feedback on what is really supportive and what is not. They tell others about the services that are available. Again, this is not transactional; it is energetic.

For years, the only childcare available to Sarah as a stay-at-home mom was the local Mother's Day Out program. She never attended the church there but she definitely spread the word, and she likes to believe her children (mostly) spread joy to the congregants who worked for the program. There is no doubt those employees spread joy to her every Tuesday and Thursday from 9:00 a.m. to 2:00 p.m.!

Here's a quick and hard reminder (for ourselves as much as for anyone else!) from one of Beth's favorite writers, Patti Digh: the best path is to make a strong offer without attaching to the outcome of that offer.[4] That's how we release ourselves from the consumer trap.

Take the example of public education. Our voices matter, not because we are consumers who are always right but because we are participants whose perspectives should be valued. However, valuing a perspective does not and cannot always mean doing what that person wants. The needs of small groups of students are sometimes more important than the desires of large majorities. There is a balance, as some of us began to understand more vividly while listening to Chana Joffe-Walt on the *New York Times'* podcast *Nice White Parents*, between advocating for our own children and valuing the system and the community it serves as a whole. That balance is a microcosm of the system that creates our schools in the first place. Public education is foundational to democracy, and long after we graduate, we can be continually educated on how to participate in democracy through our interactions with it.

It's hard not to get attached to outcomes. It can also be slightly intimidating to think about showing up with an offering in places that we need to offer something to us. We need churches to minister to us. We need to trust the public school to offer a quality education. We even need volunteer experiences to teach us something. (We have to be really careful about this one though. It can quickly lead us to transactional and exploitive mindsets.) We need civic organizations to connect us to other people.

Because of these needs, we can feel a power imbalance with these organizations, and rightly so. This is the tense, confusing truth: institutions are more powerful than we are, and all that power is derived from us.

We are entitled only to our continued participation. We are entrusted with continuing to achieve our common purpose. And we can have tremendous impact when we're willing to contribute whatever we have. While that's an uncomfortable message, it also carries tremendous relief. We don't have to do it all, and we don't have to do it all at once!

When we commit to institutions, we can see them in the context of our seasons of life. If you are still in school or just starting your career, you might have a different capacity to contribute your time than someone who recently retired. A computer programmer will share different talents with an organization than an artist. In any institution, whatever you have to offer belongs. Every institution needs a wide range of skills and talents. Every institution needs people who are willing to show up and people who are willing to write checks. Please do not discount what you have to offer. Whether your experience is in accounting, logistics, project management, human resources, caregiving, technology, marketing, teaching, leading, healing, or art, we promise that an institution needs the gifts you are willing to offer that are compatible with your season of life.

Making the Connection

Consider an institution that you're a part of or that you'd like to be a part of. How might you think about yourself as a contributor to that institution? What do you have to offer? How can you offer it in a way that's compatible with the time, money, and energy you have today?

Contributing Our Power

Contributing to institutions creates power for us, and our community institutions are perfect places to practice healthy exercises of power.

Beth: I have served on several boards for nonprofit organizations during my career. Being a director is always a weird dance for me. I'm not a good fundraiser, but I ask good questions and try to bring some helpful experiences and observations to the table. In all the years I've spent sitting in board meetings, one particular meeting stands out to me. It was the first time I voted no.

The context of my no vote doesn't matter for our purposes. Suffice it to say, the majority of the board was moving forward in a direction that made me uneasy. After a long discussion, during which I listened carefully and asked questions, a roll call vote was taken. The board chair called on me—first! I let out what might have been the longest "umm" of my life before settling into my no. I could feel the pause in the air before the next board members were called on. A series of yeses, one more no, several more yeses, and the vote concluded with me in the clear minority.

My stomach hurt for the rest of the day. I started and deleted several emails explaining and half apologizing for my vote. When I finally settled on what I wanted to say to other board members, I explained that I understood the majority position completely. I was not angry. (I truly wasn't. It surprised me how not-angry I was!) I did not expect anyone to change based on my thoughts. I was fully committed to moving on with the majority plan. I simply disagreed, and I felt obligated to express that disagreement.

Other directors followed up with me and asked for thoughts on what steps might increase my comfort level with the decision, and I responded. My suggestions weren't enacted, but they were heard. I look back at the entire process feeling satisfied. I used my voice. I hope that using my voice improved the process even though it didn't carry the day. I respected my colleagues and felt respected by them.

....

This shouldn't be a remarkable story, but it strikes us as sadly unusual. The urge to vote with the majority, especially in volunteer situations, is palpable. In nonprofits, churches, and schools, we know that people have good intentions, that they have bigger jobs than budgets, that they are sacrificing bigger salaries in the private sector to meet an endless series of needs. And so most of us who get involved in these organizations want to be unceasingly supportive.

Given that posture, disagreement doesn't surface often enough. It's there. Any collection of human beings will include conflict. We just don't voice it until it has grown to an emotionally volatile place. When someone finally vocalizes their disagreement, meetings can become tense, defensive, and hurtful. Projects can stall. Resignations can follow.

This pattern is such a waste! Think of how frequently we talk about people not feeling heard or seen. Think of what might be contributed, what opportunities might be identified, what pitfalls might be foreseen, if more people spoke out against the prevailing sentiment. In our local institutions, groupthink does not have to dominate. In these institutions, we have the most power, if we would only choose to exercise it.

These are the spaces that can teach us about healthy disagreement and holding power together so we can exercise it for common good.

It is where we can see that a vote matters, even if cast for the losing side; that dissension can change the result, even if it doesn't block the majority position; that we can grow in our respect for one another through the way that we express and handle our disagreement.

These are the places where we can develop and refine our sense of citizenship. When we move into the voting booth, our sense of participation can feel diluted by the sheer number of people participating. But in our local institutions—even when those institutions are quite large—we can feel the power we hold and the difference we make.

Disrupting the status quo might be your jam (like Sarah), or it might make you feel strained (like Beth). Either way, when you know you have something to contribute, make your contribution. Make it without expectation that it "wins." (We acknowledge that this is the hard part!) Make it because it matters. Make it because it might open up space for someone else's voice. Make it because it is your responsibility to be more than a rubber stamp. And then navigate any conflict that follows by sharing that you spoke up not because you are disconnected from the group but because you care so much.

Navigating that conflict in local institutions requires us to make the invisible visible. There can be tension and angst in these organizations because so much is assumed about one another's motivations and feelings. We think we know that the person who disagrees with us only wants attention or to control everything. We're certain that if we speak up, the chair of the meeting is going to be mad at us forever. As silly as it sounds, we all tell stories in our heads about what everyone around us is thinking and feeling. Picture a committee of people around a table with each person spinning these narratives in their minds; it's no wonder that collective action is difficult.

It's hard to know what motivates our own actions in these contexts. We definitely aren't experts in why other people are showing up as they are. When a tough issue emerges, we can invite each other to articulate our feelings and motivations so that we drop our dramatized versions of each other:

- "Hey, I'm noticing that we're all bringing quite a bit of passion to this topic, which I appreciate. It might be valuable for us to talk for a minute about what is driving us in this conversation. I'll share that I'm most interested in making sure . . ."
- "I notice that there is some tension in the room, and I think it's important to acknowledge that we are bringing very different experiences to the table. I think those differences are ultimately a strength of this [church/board/committee/group] and that talking about those differences more transparently might help us get unstuck."
- "I recognize that I'm in a different place on this issue than the majority of the group seems to be. I want you to know that I don't have any weird feelings about that and am not upset. It's just important to me to be completely candid about my perspective here. Hopefully I can add something to your thought process, even as the group moves in a different direction. I'm committed to being on the team and giving my all even though I wouldn't have chosen this option."

These are the kinds of conversations Beth had in the wake of her no vote. The short version of her vote is that Beth felt an important decision was being made by too few people—a mistake that she had made many times over in her career and that she's tried to learn from. She shared transparently that her past mistakes were sticking with her in this new context. She knew that her no might make the individuals in the small group of decision-makers feel that she didn't value them, so she explicitly told them she holds them in high regard. She knew her vote might make it seem that she wanted control in the process, so she explicitly praised the people involved and communicated that her concern was about ensuring a wide variety of voices were included. She knew she might be viewed as disgruntled following the vote, so she said plainly: "I am not upset. This is what we're here to do, and I'm excited to move forward."

These same kinds of statements are useful if you're a parent communicating with a teacher about a tough issue (or vice versa!), a church member unhappy with the new worship music (Beth's parents led the music for ages and believe her when she tells you people have feelings about this), or a volunteer having a dispute with other volunteers. We don't show up to these organizations as just parents, teachers, church members, or volunteers. We show up as the entirety of ourselves—all of our strengths married to all of our insecurities, all of our lessons learned and our naivete. We bring seemingly unrelated talents and shortcomings to these positions, and so does everyone else.

By working to make the invisible visible, we not only navigate conflict more effectively; we also uncover potential in ourselves and the people around us. "I notice" statements are helpful to work through tension. They're also helpful to drawing out the best in the people around us:

- "I've noticed that Sam has such a gift for communicating with parents. I'm wondering, Sam, if you'd be willing to lead this conversation?"

- "I'm noticing that when I feel stuck, I look to Jess for guidance, and I just wanted to share, Jess, how much I value your opinion."

- "During last year's event, I noticed that Reese went above and beyond to contribute. What do you think about asking Reese to take on greater responsibility this year?"

This is slow, patient work that can leave us feeling very exposed. There is little anonymity in our local institutions. The work of these institutions feels highly personal. Many of us have experienced the hurt that can come from that personal feeling, and we don't in any way want to diminish that hurt. We also want to see how and when we can have a healthier experience by viewing ourselves as part of the whole.

If you're reading these words and thinking about a particularly painful experience with an institution, please know that we're not encouraging you to make lifelong commitments to single organizations. In fact, we think there's a benefit to both us and institutions in some level of fluidity in how we show up. Much like that workplace garden we discussed in chapter 5, we know that we have to find the right environment in which we can flourish.

We've both been active in our churches and our school systems and our community for almost a decade now. We've fought for changes that failed. We've run for elections we lost. We've made (lots of) people mad. And here we are still showing up and still participating. We wouldn't give every experience or every institution a four-star rating. In fact, many moments inside these institutions would barely eke by with one star. Luckily, we don't look at those moments or the institutions themselves transactionally anymore. We look at the whole, and the years we've spent in connection with those in our churches and our schools and our organizations have been some of the best of our lives. We've worked together to do good that ripples out in ways we will never know.

We have faith that our individual experiences are limited, and they can't possibly capture the entirety of the institution. So, we keep doing our part and trust that others will do theirs and that together the sum will be greater than we could ever imagine. And we find that what we practice in this arena keeps us grounded as we expand outward to those with whom we share our state, our country, the internet, and the world.

NOW *What?*

As you consider where you'd like to be a contributor instead of a consumer, these questions might help you find your place:

- What issue breaks your heart when you see or hear about it? Is there a local organization working on that issue?
- What are you looking for in a community support system? There are no wrong answers here. You might want to know that if you're sick, people will bring you dinner. You might want to plug into a place with a variety of opportunities to serve the community. You

149

might want to meet people in certain fields of expertise. There are so many reasons to join community organizations, and it's important to examine what really drives you as you find your place.

- What talents do you have that are itching to be put to work? Maybe you have gifts that you aren't using in a typical day that are just what a particular institution needs. (If you have a hard time identifying your own talents, ask someone who loves you to help.)

- Who do you admire for their community participation? Ask them how they have made decisions about community involvement.

- If you're feeling stuck in a particular institution or like it might be time to reconsider your involvement, try to identify precisely what's bothering you. Is that issue a personality conflict? Is it a conflict about strategy? Is it a conflict with your values? What would need to change in you or in the institution to help? Is that change available?

7

Local and State Government

Culture Wars and Poop

Sarah: In 2015, I knocked on over five thousand doors and asked my fellow Paducahans to vote for me for city commission. I'll never forget the week before election day when an early voter informed me she had already voted for me. It was at that moment that I began to believe I might actually win my election. I was a young liberal woman trying to win in ruby-red Kentucky and, even though I was running for the nonpartisan city commission, I was also watching the presidential race between Hillary Clinton and Donald Trump and realizing the visceral partisan anger ran deeper than I wanted to acknowledge. On election day, I was prepared to lose but comfort myself with Hillary Clinton's win.

Instead, on election night, I realized I had won at almost the exact moment I realized I would be sharing my victory night with Donald Trump. Bittersweet doesn't begin to cover it, but I realize now that it was the perfect introduction to my new role. Nothing is pure in local politics, including victories.

I envisioned elected office as the summit. I'd reached the top and now I would be able to enact the policies I knew would help the people of my town. Instead, I was sworn in and realized I was, in fact, at the bottom of the hill and that I'd have to learn the steep turns and craggy switchbacks to make even the tiniest bit of progress. And despite losing my reelection campaign two years later (insert Garth singing "Unanswered Prayers" here), we did make progress on hard issues like banning the confederate flag from the Veterans Day parade and bringing recycling to the city and passing a Fairness Ordinance.

But when I look back on my term, it's not the big issues that make for good Facebook fodder where I learned the most. I learned the most from poop.

As a city commissioner, I was appointed to our local sewer board, and it was that experience that I still carry with me. Learning about our combined sewer system, I gained a deeper understanding and empathy for past city leaders and how our current choices impact future generations. Seeing the impact of federal regulation on local municipalities, I developed a deep respect for the complexities that come from sharing a pipe or a drain or an entire river with thousands (or millions) of your fellow citizens. Watching the way some people treated sanitary workers or the sanitary system itself, I learned that we have lost the ability to see government functioning on the ground—or below the ground—in our everyday lives.

For too many of us, we hear *government* and immediately think *national political debate.* In so many ways, we use the words interchangeably. We fight about too much government or too little government, and in the same conversation, we complain about political advertising and the opposing party. We use Washington, DC, or *the swamp* interchangeably with the word *government,* as if the federal government encompasses the totality of governance in our lives. We show up in very different numbers for presidential elections vs. *off-cycle* elections. (The term itself tells you what we think about elections in which we're still electing public officers for hugely consequential positions.) But the government is so much more than the political partisan narratives we perpetuate about it. It's easy to see that in our communities.

Government is the roads you drive on—both the interstate highways, paved and maintained by the federal government, and the roads you drive on every day—some maintained by city road crews and some maintained by our states. Government is the school your child attends that is funded by local taxes collected by the state and then redistributed to your district and subsidized further by federal tax dollars. Government is the label your local pharmacist places on your prescription to warn you of side effects and the state regulatory agency that licensed that pharmacy to run. Government is the fire department that opens up hydrants during the dog days of summer and the public library that offers a warm place of refuge during a snowstorm. Government is the public utilities that light your homes, fill your glasses, and, yes, flush and filter your poop. (And, please, if you take nothing else from this book, know that flushable wipes are not in fact flushable!)

Government Is How We Live Together

Just like with our societal institutions, a consumer mentality can infect how we see government. It's become a product—a one-dimensional thing—that we treat like consumers, instead of an organization of all of us together trying to fulfill a purpose. We pay taxes, so we begin to expect certain things in return. But a democracy is not transactional, and it takes seeing the up-close-and-personal functioning of government to appreciate that.

Beth: My friend Jen lives two houses down from us. Our houses are situated on a cul-de-sac, and from my backyard, I can see the open field that sits behind Jen's house. That field is outside the subdivision, and Jen stays in communication with the people who own it. I was recording a podcast one morning when I saw a text pop up from Jen. The owner of the field was burning a brush pile uncomfortably close to Jen's backyard. She works from home, so she was able to keep a close eye on it. A few more texts shared that the fire had gotten bigger and smokier but then seemed to be dying down.

About an hour later, Chad and I were eating lunch and hearing about Ellen's half day at kindergarten when Jen texted again: "Shed caught fire. Fire dept on their way."

The fire had grown and engulfed a small black barn that sat behind another neighbor's home. We walked outside and saw it collapse. Our neighbor's fence caught on fire. It's hard to grasp how quickly a fire spreads until you witness it. We stood, transfixed, until Ellen walked outside, saw the fire, and said, "I don't think I should be involved with this."

The fire department arrived in less than five minutes. They quickly had the fire under control and started taking the rest of the barn apart to ensure that the flames were completely extinguished. Three trucks lined the cul-de-sac. My neighbor Karen grabbed Ellen and took her up front to see the flurry of activity around them.

I remembered that a few nights before, Ellen caught a piece of a conversation Chad and I were having about filing our taxes. She had asked why we pay taxes, and we had done maybe a C+ job answering. (We're human! It's hard to be on your A game as you're contemplating what you might owe this year.)

I walked around to where Karen was holding Ellen, who was watching the hoses being wrapped up. "Ellen," I said, "remember when we were talking about taxes the other night?" Of course she did. How dare I suggest otherwise? (Ellen has a real vibe.) "Taxes are how this happened. Without taxes, we'd be on our own figuring out how to get this fire out safely. These firefighters were able to come so quickly on these trucks and use this water in the fire hydrant because of taxes. Taxes pay their salaries and for their training and their uniforms."

Ellen considered this for a while. "Even their hats?"

"Even their hats."

....

Beth's neighbor doesn't owe more in taxes now that they've called on the services of the fire department. And Beth and Ellen saw their tax dollars (OK, Beth's dollars) at work in real and impactful ways, even though the fire wasn't in their yard. Politics is winner-takes-all in so many ways, but governance is not. The entire community benefits when a fire is put out (just ask London) or from a sanitary sewer (man, London learned that lesson the hard way for all of us as well!). The infrastructure provided by the government is also the foundation upon which our economy runs. Businesses can grow and thrive when they can depend on safe roads to deliver inventory and customers to their doors. We all depend on the electricity that flows when we flip a switch and the water that runs when we turn a knob. The interconnectedness of our lives is intense, and it is the government that tends to the pragmatic reality of those connections.

Making the Connection

In 2021, we published a summer series called "Infrastructure in Real Life" on *Pantsuit Politics*. Preparing for that series, we learned to "see the matrix." Government shows up everywhere in essential and luxurious ways. Where do you see government at work in your home and on your street? (This is a really fun exercise to share with the kids in your life!)

We Need More Local News

Training ourselves to see that reality at the local level helps us filter some of the noise of national politics. But the nationalization of politics (and the erasure of governance) isn't simply about our individual mindsets.

Many other societal and cultural forces have led us to where we are. The framers of our Constitution were responding to the failure of the Articles of the Confederation and Perpetual Union. Why had those Articles, agreed to by our original thirteen states, failed? State identity dominated in the country, and the federal government was too weak to be effective. We didn't have too much national politics. We had too little. Can you imagine?

Until the mid-twentieth century, state political parties dominated the political scene. State political parties and the party bosses who ran them offered more than marketing to voters. They trafficked in political power—not the performance of power through cultural grievance, but actual power. As in: they got you a job or made sure your trash ran on time or that the police didn't ignore your neighborhood. They decided who ran in primaries and introduced them to all the right fundraisers and then demanded loyalty in return. Now, no one is arguing that party bosses and the patronage system were the golden age of American politics. Many of the mechanisms of party power were greased with a lot of money and corruption. But, as we see with Congress recently voting to bring back pork barrel spending, having something to exchange to grease the wheels of power (besides a cruel tweet or cable news shout-out) is helpful.

With the end of the patronage system, the party bosses of the nineteenth century finally began to fall from power. Modern media and marketing began to replace the state and local political networks on which politicians previously depended to reach voters. Around the same time, local media began to struggle, making it more difficult for Americans to follow the governance of their local communities (both good and bad).

A great way to understand how less local media affects the way we see the government is by looking at the elimination of the Fairness Doctrine (aka one of the secrets to Rush

Limbaugh's success).[1] From 1949 to 1987, the Federal Communications Commission required licensed broadcasters to devote some portion of airtime to matters of public interest and to present contrasting viewpoints about those matters. Broadcasters weren't required to give equal time to contrasting views, but they were required to expose audiences to diversity of thought. The Fairness Doctrine eroded during the Reagan years, and some argue that its absence has led to the erosion of first, civility, and second, truth.

The Fairness Doctrine, however effective it might have been, would not apply to the endless cable and streaming options that dominate viewing habits today. With the advent of social media, more news intake is curated by algorithms than editors, further increasing the nationalization of . . . well, everything. The same technology that decimated local media let national polarization flourish by elevating certain influential voices (including some of the same ones in right-wing partisan media) and silencing others.[2] As national media became more influential, especially on our social networks, national politics became the stand-in for all our concerns about government.

This history helps us orient ourselves to the present. Today, over sixty-five million Americans live in counties with only one local newspaper—or no newspaper at all.[3] In Beth's hometown, for example, a local paper for the entire county is published one time every week. It contains a few truly local stories but is largely filled with syndicated content from the national publishing group that owns it. Sarah is lucky enough to have a daily local newspaper, and still the letters to the editors are often about national politics because the local paper is certainly not everyone's sole source of news!

We can't celebrate the success of a new local infrastructure project if there's no local paper there to cover it. A renovated public library or expanded access at a public school isn't going to make the national news, which is all many Americans see. Individual community successes are more likely to be trumpeted in national media if they came from private—not governmental—effort. A lack of local media also means we miss vigorous reporting about local government accountability. That leaves gossip, jealousy, rumor, and innuendo to fill in the gaps, dissuading people who might otherwise be excellent public officials from serving.

Making the Connection

Examine your own local news environment:

- Do you have a local newspaper? When was the last time you read it?
- How much do you depend on social media for your local news? How do you find out about the success stories (not just the failures) in your local community?
- Do you have any skills you can bring to this issue? You don't have to be a journalist. Could you simply share a positive experience you had on the job with your local government? We're predisposed to complain. Can you focus on sharing something that left you feeling optimistic about your local community?

Home Is Where the Power Is

Motivating voters to vote in local races without good local information is difficult. So opponents link their incumbents to national polarizing figures. What's easier, after all—explaining the intricacies of the budget process and how your opponent exploited them OR just throwing up a photoshopped picture of them next to Nancy Pelosi? When Beth's dad ran for judge executive of his home county, he was asked more about abortion than parks, and Sarah was asked most about her presidential pick.

> **If we want healthier national politics, we have to let some decisions exist outside it.**

Power is fundamentally transactional, but by nationalizing politics, we've replaced transactionalism with consumerism. The parties as brokers of power (flawed as that system was) offered people something concrete. Now, the parties are brands. State and local parties traffic less in offering a road project or good trash service and more in symbolic gestures, like censuring national officials who buck the party line. Expressions of displeasure or enthusiasm from the state parties don't actually serve the public. But because local government is invisible and state party leadership is nearly extinct outside of election cycles, politicians and voters double down on the "all politics is national" approach.

If we want healthier national politics, we have to let some decisions exist outside it. That requires a greater connection to what's happening at home.

Beth: I'm guilty of devoting the bulk of my civic attention to national politics. I love a Supreme Court decision, a cromnibus, even a presidential election. My state political knowledge has been woefully inadequate, especially since I moved to northern Kentucky and have been engaged in the greater Cincinnati community. Consequently, my sense of identity as a Kentuckian has been watered down. I sit on the boards of Ohio-based nonprofits. I've received awards with *Cincinnati* and *Ohio* in the titles. I'm ashamed to say I haven't even watched much Kentucky basketball for several years.

COVID-19 brought me back to my old Kentucky home in a powerful, wholly unexpected way. In the very early days of the pandemic, Kentucky's governor, Andy Beshear, began offering a daily briefing. It was unlike anything I had seen before. Media covered these briefings, but they were very clearly not for media. They were for Kentuckians.

Governor Beshear shared stories of how Kentuckians were helping one another through COVID-19. He showed videos of choirs singing over Zoom and montages of sidewalk art from across the state. An American Sign Language interpreter, Virginia Moore, accompanied the governor for many of these briefings, and I'm not exaggerating when I say that she was probably one of Kentucky's most beloved and popular figures at that point.

I looked forward to seeing the ways Kentuckians were adapting to the pandemic, and I held my breath when Governor Beshear reached the moment of announcing how many Kentuckians had been lost to COVID-19 that day. The governor displayed a shocking amount of emotion for a politician. His daily grief was real, as was his pride in sharing how Kentuckians were sharing food, making masks, and sending cards to people in skilled nursing facilities. His frustration was apparent over the difficulty in meeting the significant demands on unemployment insurance. His anger was obvious when superspreader events were held in defiance of state guidelines.

Looking back, those displays of emotion created a stronger sense of state affiliation in me than anything has in my lifetime. Hearing daily from my governor about a shared struggle, seeing my own emotions reflected in and through him, and cheering on his efforts with like-minded friends and neighbors gave me a very deep sense that I am a Kentuckian, and that being a Kentuckian means something. I believed Governor Beshear when he said, every day, "We will get through this together." I want to keep getting through together.

....

Some of the nationalization of politics is here to stay. As Beth's experience reflects, our identities are less rooted in what state we were born in (except for Texas; y'all are special) than they were at the founding of the country when most people lived and died in one state. We're not going back to that way of life, and that's fine. We all might move several times over the course of our lives, but our connections to the cities, counties, and states where we live *now* and the people who live there with us still matter.

Sarah: My devotion to my hometown of Paducah is well-known for regular listeners of our show. Beth calls me a one-woman visitor's bureau. I love living here, and I can expound enthusiastically on its many virtues for hours. And yet, like so many people, teenage Sarah couldn't wait to get away. I wanted to get away from Paducah and head to Washington, DC. My family visited when I was in middle school, and I had been besotted ever since. My best friend, who went with us on the trip, remembers me standing on a hill in Arlington National Cemetery, looking over the district, and exclaiming dreamily, "I'm going to live here one day."

And I did. My husband and I lived in Washington, DC, for five years, and I still think of it as my second home. I took my first breath in Paducah, Kentucky, but in so many ways Washington, DC, made me who I am. I'm so grateful for my time there because there is nothing that can replace seeing the government run up close and personal. I worked in the United States Senate and called the Capitol my workplace. I gave tours and watched lawmakers walk the halls. (I even shared an elevator with Senator Ted Kennedy once!) I drafted legislation and stood on the Senate floor and stayed in constant awe of my surroundings. Anyone who has worked in a city hall or state capitol can probably understand my experience. There is something so special in witnessing the mundane. The big fancy buildings that fill our television screens (or Facebook feeds), as pundits rail against politics or politicians or policy, are just buildings—buildings filled with people just like me. In fact, it was me for a moment in time. There were no grand schemes or designs. I didn't witness anything except some people doing their best and some people working out their demons. And I try to keep that in mind when I hear conversations about "those blockheads in DC" or "those idiots in Frankfort." I was them. They are me. Washington, DC, is both incredibly special and just like every other place I've lived in a million little ways.

....

In a way, the fact that so many of us will move several times over the course of our lives brings an empowering perspective to our understanding of government. As we change locations, we bring new experiences and perspectives. We can see the different ways different cities and counties and states solve their problems. We can see the pros and cons of different forms of government and different types of leadership.

We can let those connections and insights fuel the ways we interact with the place we live right now. And we can help without running for office ourselves, donating to campaigns, or knocking on doors! If those are your gifts, our hats are off to you! And if they are not, you have a place in local politics. There are so many ways that you can contribute.

- We can recognize that our local road department does do a good job and brag on them at our next gathering. Even better, we can send them an actual note (or a cookie cake—we *believe* in the power of cookie cake). Our local municipal employees are the unsung heroes of our daily lives, as well as the people who run our parks departments and inspect our businesses and, yes, even collect our taxes. They go unrecognized and unappreciated.

- We can join our local boards and committees. A massive amount of work in our cities, counties, and states is done by the boards and committees that hear zoning applications and run our local libraries and license professionals across our states.

- We can go to these board meetings and realize that change comes from joining with others, not attempting to control the outcome.
- We can become a precinct chair and join our state political parties. We can do this even if we think of ourselves as more centrist or independent. Parties need influence from people representing a broad spectrum of ideological intensity.
- We can write a social media post telling our neighbors about the candidates running for office and encouraging people to vote in local elections.
- And we can unite in our communities and states in the face of shared struggle.

The water, the roads, the schools, the fire department, the poop . . . these seemingly mundane services that we take for granted might be our way out of the culture wars. Perhaps a prior generation or two were able to take vital services for granted. We cannot. Our infrastructure has aged to the point of needing serious investment. The climate has changed and continues changing in ways that require system upgrades to both operate in the new reality and hold off a more devastated future. These issues are lasting and pivotal to every movement. Whether your passion is racial justice, reducing poverty, eliminating homelessness, or realizing more entrepreneurial opportunities, the work of state and local governments is crucial to a functioning today and a brighter tomorrow.

NOW *What?*

Consider what is working well in your local community. What leaders have influenced that success? How might you recognize their efforts and encourage them to expand on those strengths? Try this same exercise at the state level.

A simple thank-you note is a contribution. Where else might you contribute to your state or local politics?

8

National Politics

You Deal with Your Pain Your Way, I Deal with My Pain Mine

Sarah: I am a victim of gun violence. In 1997 a freshman at my high school opened fire on a prayer circle gathered before the bell rang. He killed three of my fellow classmates and wounded six others. For years, it was hard to call myself a victim because I wasn't among the nine people physically wounded that day. I wasn't even in the school building but had just entered it when my classmates flooded out in shock. Since I thought I didn't have any "real" recovery or healing to deal with, I channeled my emotions into anger at a system I felt had failed to protect me and my classmates. When I was in college my mom and I flew to Washington, DC, for the Million Mom March calling for stricter gun laws. I went to law school and worked on Capitol Hill—all the time continuing to advocate for gun control and all the time continuing to watch the list of mass shootings grow and grow.

On the twentieth anniversary of the shooting at my high school, I gathered with several of my classmates. We all shared our stories, our grief, and our trauma. We began to connect more on Facebook as well, and I realized that one of my classmates was a passionate gun owner and advocate. There was absolutely no way for me to be angry at her. I had listened to her stories from that day. I knew that her own child had been attending another local high school that recently experienced a shooting, just two decades after our own. She was experiencing multigenerational school shootings. How could I angrily discard her—as abhorrent as I found her political positions—as uncaring in the face of violence and death?

The trauma of that day and how it affected both of us is more complicated than our policy positions on gun control. It took me a long time and a lot of therapy to realize that I was also a victim on December 1, 1997. Being traumatized at such a young age taught me that life is finite and precarious, and it also left me with intense anxiety that someone I love will die violently and tragically. Being traumatized by someone who was also very young taught me that villainizing those who do evil things isn't the path to understanding and also left me angry at people who refuse to see their impact on others. For so long, I felt immense pressure to do something for my classmates who lost their lives. I thought that was gun control, but under that rubric I have failed. Under that rubric I care about my classmates, and my friend who opposes gun control doesn't, even though one of the victims that day was her best friend. So I have had to abandon that rubric. Not because I don't still believe that real gun control is essential and could save lives. I do. I just can't tie my humanity or anyone else's to their position on it. I couldn't see my way out of the maze of my own trauma for so long. How can I possibly judge the way others are lost?

....

A maze of trauma feels like an apt metaphor for the United States some (most) days. We are both celebrating our fortieth years as we write this book, and we could mark the milestones of our lives with the national traumas we've witnessed along the way: the beating of Rodney King, the Oklahoma City bombing, the OJ Simpson trial, Columbine, 9/11, the Iraq and Afghanistan Wars, Hurricane Katrina, Sandy Hook, the 2016 election, the Las Vegas shooting, the killing of George Floyd, a global pandemic, and the January 6, 2021, insurrection.

Each of these events could be accompanied by many more. George Floyd was not the only Black man to be killed by the police. He's not even the only one who lost his life on video in 2020. The school shootings and mass shootings we left *off* the list could fill the rest of this chapter. If the OJ Simpson trial was a trauma, weren't we also affected by the murders of JonBenét Ramsey and Laci Peterson? It's impossible to talk about the Oklahoma City bombing without also talking about Ruby Ridge and Waco. When Hurricane Katrina hit, watching California burn wasn't yet an annual occurrence, and the people of Houston, many of whom moved *from* New Orleans, weren't experiencing winter blackouts. And the wars in Iraq and Afghanistan are now a fraction of our long, complicated, and dangerous military presence in that area of the world.

Making the Connection

Think back to a national trauma that had a profound impact on you. Can you move beyond just where you were when you found out to how it still impacts you today? Did it change forever how you saw the government or another institution? How did it impact how you saw your fellow citizens?

So, what does all that national trauma mean for the country as a whole and the citizens contained within it? After all, we're a big country with a lot of people. The United States covers about 3.7 million square miles. That makes it about the same size as China and larger than every country in the world except Russia and Canada. Just over 331 million people live in the United States, which puts it behind China and India in terms of population—both of which have a billion more people than the United States. It also is among the world's wealthiest countries by any metric. We are big, we are populous, and we are powerful.

There is, simply put, a lot going on in the country that we call home, and a lot of what is going on and what has gone on is painful.

The Role of Trauma

Over the past several decades we've come a long way in our understanding of trauma and how it affects us as individuals. One of the biggest breakthroughs has been adverse childhood experiences, which California's surgeon general Dr. Nadine

Burke Harris described "as big as germ theory."[1] Our understanding of ACEs comes from a massive survey conducted in the 1990s by Kaiser Permanente, which studied the effect of adverse childhood experiences on adult health. Every person was given a single point for abuse, neglect, or other traumatic childhood experiences, including divorce. People who experience abuse or neglect or dysfunction in the home as kids are more likely to have health problems later in life, ranging from depression to heart disease.[2] The higher their ACEs score, the higher the probability for chronic disease later in life. It makes you wonder what the United States ACEs score would be. We've listed the national traumas from our forty years of life, but some of what seems so painful in the country right now is that we are also facing earlier traumas—*founding traumas*—and their ongoing impact.

Trauma experienced during childhood is so damaging because children are both extremely vulnerable and extremely limited in how they react to stress and pain. Sarah once had a therapist tell her that's why experiencing trauma as a child is so hard. As one gains additional skills and maturity, reprocessing the trauma becomes necessary. This feels like what the United States is experiencing right now. We grow older and gain a deeper, more complex understanding of our history and are forced to confront the traumas anew.

Our Founding Traumas

In this country's infancy, we were vulnerable. We were vulnerable to other nations, and we were vulnerable to internal disputes. Our framers put forth a promise in the Constitution that "all men are created equal, that they are endowed by their Creator with certain unalienable Rights, that among these are Life, Liberty and the pursuit of Happiness." But in the face of vulnerability and fear, they chose to traumatize many to protect that promise for a select few. They chose continued enslavement for hundreds of thousands of Americans until that promise and the relationship built upon it was almost completely severed during the Civil War.

Post–Civil War, we began to see more and more Americans fight for their right to claim that promise as their own, and yet the traumas continued. In 1931, James Truslow Adams coined the phrase "American Dream." He wrote, "It is not a dream of motor cars and high wages merely, but a dream of social order in which each man and each woman shall be able to attain to the fullest stature of which they are innately capable, and recognized by others for what they are, regardless of the fortuitous circumstances of their birth."[3] Millions of Americans over the past hundred years have followed that dream only to be discriminated against, shunned, abused, or murdered because of their race, ethnicity, sex, gender, or sexual orientation. Progress has been made without a doubt, but with every moment of progress come more voices calling the traumas both recent and old to our national consciousness.

We gain clarity and maturity and see the depth of pain anew. And, of course, in a country of about 331 million people, the level of complexity along that journey can at times seem infinite. Many of us are not seeing the trauma with new eyes because we have been experiencing it for generations. Many of us are refusing to recognize the trauma at all because our power and security stands firmly on the foundation of the status quo. But the national traumas of enslavement and tribal genocide and war are forever a part of every American's story, whether we want to acknowledge them or not. And the more recent traumas of watching our fellow citizens die at the hands of the police or recounting story after story of sexual assault or suffering from COVID-19 not only call forth those past traumas but layer new trauma on top of our own individual histories of suffering.

In light of all this compounding trauma, it is not surprising that polarization has flourished—hurt people hurt people, as the saying goes. That polarization has turned the traumas themselves into fertile ground for the latest culture war. In 2019, the *New York Times* used the four hundredth anniversary of the first enslaved people to arrive in America to launch The 1619 Project, which aims, in the words of its founder, Nikole Hannah-Jones, to "reframe the country's history by placing the consequences of slavery and the contributions of Black Americans at the very center of the United States' national narrative."[4] While The 1619 Project is not without its critics (both sincere and not), Hannah-Jones and those who joined her argue for that progression of grief and understanding. We've got more tools now to deal with this trauma. We've got new empowered and impacted voices in the conversation. We've got new technologies to make it accessible to more people. Let's grieve and examine and illuminate this national trauma anew.

As with any trauma, everyone has different coping mechanisms. While some Americans are ready and willing to face these traumas, some Americans leaned all the way into compartmentalization and denial. The 1619 Project became the punching bag of right-wing media and suddenly critical race theory was the newest culture battleground. The Trump administration decided to form an advisory committee that produced *The 1776 Report*, an ahistorical pushback on critical race theory and The 1619 Project, for more "patriotic" education.

Part of this reaction is inevitable in our individualistic culture that teaches us to see pain as weakness and victimization as a moral failing. We have a long history of silencing and belittling victims in this country because the victim reminds us of our own pain and our own vulnerability.

We are going to continue to fight about statues, monuments, curriculum, cancelation, and displays of patriotism. On many levels, it's important that we have vigorous disagreement about our telling of history and our commemoration of historic figures. As America ages, our understanding of our nation should become more complex. There's something to celebrate in debating the stories we tell, the relationships between stories and storytellers, and what constitutes knowledge worth spreading.

It is also important that these debates remain intellectually honest. There are academic criticisms of The 1619 Project that ought to be held alongside the *New York Times*'s work. There are also textbooks throughout the United States that fail students by omitting crucial pieces of our country's history. There are bills passing state legislatures and boards of education across the country attempting to shield students from any discomfort associated with America's founding. Intellectual honesty must flow in all directions as we seek a deeper understanding of where we've been and where we are as a nation. And intellectual honesty requires us to do better than an overly simplistic theory of history that sorts out heroes and villains.

We Are More Than Our Labels

Beth: When we started *Pantsuit Politics* in 2015, we were "Sarah from the left" and "Beth from the right." In hindsight, "Beth from the right" was a tough label for me to carry from the beginning. I squeezed into the Republican label like jeans that you really want to fit. My understanding of what it meant to be a Republican didn't line up well with the modern Republican party, but I was fixated in that understanding. I like local problem-solving. I prefer private solutions to public solutions when private solutions are available. I think the state has too much power, especially when it's exercising that power vis-à-vis individuals.

That stuff probably worked under the Republican banner, but the GOP was turning its focus far away from those tenets to focus on issues where I was badly misaligned. I don't believe that abortion should be illegal. I support marriage equality. I abhor attempts to restrict the rights of transgender people. I think immigration is culturally and economically good. And I believe it's as important to examine America's fundamental sins as it is to celebrate America's resounding successes.

When the Republican Party nominated Donald Trump for president, I felt lost. When Donald Trump became the president, I was embarrassed and unmoored. In the early days of his administration, President Trump issued executive orders limiting immigration, and the Department of Homeland Security separated families at the southern border to "deter" immigration.

These policies were completely inconsistent with my beliefs about what America is supposed to be and do. As Sarah and I traveled around the country to speak to college students, business leaders, and churches, I felt like I was constantly explaining my party affiliation: "I'm a Republican, but not this kind."

My heart started to sink every time I heard or read "Beth from the right." Listeners "from the right" sent me angry emails about how poorly I represented them. Reviewers on iTunes complained that our branding was misleading. I still feel nauseated thinking about everything I felt, read, and internalized during those years.

I changed my party registration on my phone in July 2019 after hearing President Trump say that Representatives Talib, Omar, Ocasio-Cortez, and Pressley should "go back" where they came from. Something about that moment (and the utter failure of the Republican Party to reject his language, not just in that instance but over and over) struck me: I was not a Republican, and I probably wouldn't be ever again.

Now I wear the Democratic label the same uncomfortable way. These jeans don't fit well either. I think the reason I feel better about wearing them relates to the way I process our national traumas. I'm so proud to be an American. I love this country. And I want us to acknowledge where we've gone wrong. I want us to want to do better. Sometimes the way Democrats want to go about doing better feels all wrong to me. I'm more comfortable with feeling like the solutions are wrong, I guess, than feeling like we can't agree on the problems.

"Life is hard though," I can hear my former Republican voice saying. "The government can't fix everything." That's not wrong. The reality of living in this century is that government is so intertwined in our lives, it is rarely neutral. When it comes to how we treat one another, I want a government that is willing to recognize how even matters of the distant past still hurt my fellow citizens today.

....

Just as we want to sort ourselves by party labels that can be ill-fitting, we also seem to want to force every person and group into a false binary—victim or villain. So, if you don't want to "play the victim," then your only other option is to adopt the defensive posture of someone accused of villainy. You either acknowledge weakness or project strength on behalf of yourself or your group.

Of course, some of us are victims and some of us are villains, but we are never *just* those things. And trauma—be it abuse inside a family or wars between nation-states—affects both the perceived victim and the perceived villain. Nothing is lost in acknowledging this pain, and nothing is condoned by recognizing that the acknowledgment itself is hard.

However, in the political space where so much is wrapped up in our identity, acknowledging that our very country is both a victim and a villain can feel impossible. So, it becomes easier to assert that our country is always the victim or always the villain. We were victims of British imperialism or Soviet sabotage who always persevered, and therefore we are victims no longer but heroes. Those who see things differently are the real villains. OR we were always villains perpetuating genocide and theft from Native Americans or slavery or disenfranchisement or economic inequality, and those who refuse to acknowledge that are the present-day villains.

The difficult reality is that America, like most other countries on this planet, is a complex mix of victim, villain, AND hero because no country is without trauma, and trauma makes victims, villains, and heroes of us all. We fall victim to abuse and harm and neglect through no fault of our own. We take out our pain on others in villainous ways. We also integrate our suffering and self-awareness in ways that are truly heroic.

Upholding Each Other's Dignity

Political theorist Judith Shklar argued that the painful process of prioritizing the voices of the victims is in fact essential to a functioning democracy. In her book *The Faces of Injustice*, she wrote, "When we attempt to make political decisions about what to do in specific instances of injustice, we must give the victim's voice its full weight. This is in keeping with the best impulses of democracy and is our only alternative to a complacency that is bound to favor the unjust."[5] It seems to us that Shklar is not arguing for the prioritization of victimization but rather making sure that the trauma we inevitably inflict upon one another in a country of 331 million people stays ever-present in our minds, our conversations, and our policies.

We've spent this book asking you to see the people and connections around you more clearly—to see the expectations surrounding conflict in the argument with your dad, to see where vulnerability is keeping you away from neighbors, to see how you treat institutions as products to consume.

We're asking you now to see our national political discourse through the lens of pain.

We cannot control our fellow citizens, and we certainly cannot heal their pain. However, how we deal with our shared trauma in our interactions with one another will be our legacy. Through years of podcasting about the most difficult topics in American life, we have found few simple rules that apply universally. There is almost always an exception. There are almost always complications and fresh perspectives and opportunities to change our minds. We always try to reject easy certainty.

However, the one rule we never waver from is that we do not dehumanize.

There are no garbage humans—no matter how easy that tweet is to write. We lean into humanity—at all costs. Humanization can be as simple as saying, "I see your pain." That doesn't mean I condone your actions. That doesn't mean I do not believe you to be a danger to myself and others. That certainly doesn't mean I have to vote for you or agree with you or invite you into my life (or social media feed). It simply means I see that you have a heart that beats beneath your chest and that heart is capable of breaking . . . just like mine.

Making the Connection

Think about a family or friend or community member who is on the other side of the political debate from you. How could national trauma have impacted them? Were they watching the violence of Vietnam on their TV screen every night? Did they start active shooter drills in kindergarten? How can you look at their politics through the lens of pain?

Pain, Polarization, and Progress

Acknowledging our country's traumas will not solve polarization. Seeing the pain that lies behind power-grabs and hate and oppression will not provide justice or protection or healing to those who have been harmed. However, denying that trauma and pain won't either. America has made hard-fought progress over the past two hundred years, and not a single step of that progress began with dehumanization. In fact, our greatest moments of progress—the moments in American history the world looks to in admiration—always began because, among a complex mix of motivations, our shared humanity won the day. Universal suffrage. The Civil Rights movement. Our National Parks system. The Americans with Disabilities Act. There was nothing pure about these victories, but there is something essential in their impacts. We are attempting to grow the world's first multicultural democracy, and our moments of growth are sown with hard work not hatred. A soil hardened with hatred for our fellow citizens will starve the roots before a single bud can bloom.

> A soil hardened with hatred for our fellow citizens will starve the roots before a single bud can bloom.

As big and broken as we can sometimes be, we still believe that this American ideal offers promise. It's not the belonging offered by a national ethnicity, which America never was and never will be. It's the promise of that idea that James Truslow Adams so beautifully described when he coined the phrase "the American Dream." That each citizen can be "recognized by others for *what they are*"—fully human and connected to the whole.

NOW What?

What role has trauma played in your politics? Where can you see pain present in our national political debates?

9

Social Media

Twitter Ain't Church, but a Group Might Be Good for Your Soul

Sarah: I have worked online in some capacity since 2011. Before then, everything I did online was a hobby. My husband had started our personal blog when we got married in 2003, and I took over in 2009 when our first son was born. We posted stories and photos, but it was mainly for family and friends. Then my former law school classmate Sarah asked if I would be interested in starting a mommy blog with her. I'll be forever grateful that Sarah saw something worthwhile in my writing and envisioned a professional future for the two of us in the online space. She saw something I couldn't possibly have imagined from my little life in Paducah.

I worked on the mommy blog with Sarah for several years and translated my new skills into social media consulting for businesses in my small town until my husband convinced me to start a podcast. Then I got the opportunity to reach out to Beth and pay forward what Sarah had done for me: recognize that she had something special and offer up a vision.

Not one single step in the path that brought me to this point would have been possible without social media. Sarah saw what I wrote because I shared it on Facebook, which is where we then shared and grew our blog. My social media consulting business was built on helping businesses navigating Facebook and then Instagram. Beth saw my posts on Facebook and asked if I'd be interested in a guest post. Our podcast grew tremendously at the start because Apple Podcasts tweeted about us, and we built community through live tweeting the various presidential primary debates way back in 2015.

And it's not just professional opportunities. My skin looks better (follow me here, I promise it's related). Several years ago, Jamie B. Golden started showing up in my Insta stories sharing skin-care tips. At the time, I had a firmly entrenched narrative that I didn't care about beauty influencers or beauty really at all. But Jamie was a pop culture podcaster I admired, which is probably why she and her ten-step K-beauty routine were able to snake their way into my heart (and Ulta shopping cart). Jamie made me laugh and helped me learn the difference between a good sheet mask and a bad sheet mask, why I need Vitamin A, B, *and* C, and why I actually did care about beauty and skin care, after all. Eventually, I tricked her into chatting with me on Voxer, and now I consider her a friend and one of my most trusted professional advisors. (If you think she knows skin care, you should hear her wax poetic on engagement analytics.)

I have met Jamie once in person. ONCE. (For now, I've got lots of plans to hang out with her post-pandemic style.)

That's the power of social media. And while I could also write several pages on the heartbreak I have experienced, one-sided stories aren't really stories at all—they're just opinions. At this point, so many of us have a long and complicated story with social media—full of connection and disconnection. Hopefully, the next ten years will contain more of the former than the latter.

．．．．．．．．．．．．．．．．．．．．．．．．．

You might be surprised that we're opening with a positive story about social media. We don't have on rose-colored glasses. Social media deserves much of the bad rep it gets. It contributes to paranoia, conspiracy theories, shame spirals, bullying, harassment, mob mentality, irrational markets, and groupthink. On top of all that, the business model, as it develops over time, is ethically disturbing.

Dr. Shoshana Zuboff's *The Age of Surveillance Capitalism: The Fight for a Human Future at the New Frontier of Power* details the ways tech companies decide what is known and by whom, which is creating a new and extreme form of inequality. She compellingly connects this extreme imbalance to political chaos and epistemic dominance, as "democratic governance is replaced by computational governance."[1] Her take on the events of January 6, 2021, is extraordinarily helpful in understanding the Capitol insurrection. It also feels disturbingly prescient, describing the science fiction novel that it feels like we're living and creating every day.

If you ask us, most days we'd both say the costs of social media outweigh the benefits, and it's time to make dramatic changes. We are carefully following the work of technological ethicists, policymakers, sociologists, and cyberpsychologists as they continue to help us understand what social media is and how it changes us. We're equal parts concerned, angry, sad, and fascinated by how, in our lifetimes, the social fabric has been drastically altered by our ability to like, share, and click.

Our Social Media Reality

In this chapter, we're going to leave the details of that evolution to the experts and accept the realities of today: (1) social media exists, (2) our listeners and readers use it frequently, (3) it meets some human needs that aren't being met in other ways, and (4) it presents all kinds of opportunities and challenges around political dialogue. For our purposes, social media is a part of life that, at least for now, we are expected to navigate individually, from our positions of relative ignorance about all that happens behind the screen and inside our brains as we scroll.

We've often said that social media is a tool that can be used to build or tear down, create or destroy. As our understanding of social media deepens, that metaphor's fit diminishes. Talking about social media as a tool implies that we wield control over its use. We know now that total control is impossible. Perhaps a better metaphor is thinking of social media as space—a galaxy filled with planets we might visit, black holes *for sure*, and constellations that feel closer than they should. We're flying around this galaxy, recognizing some well-traveled areas, knowing that there are uncharted frontiers all around us.

Context Is the Best Policy

As we decide where to "go," we've noticed a pattern. The healthiest spaces on social media for us are wrapped in context. People visit these spaces for defined reasons that are well understood. They share some characteristics. Some explicit or unspoken but well-understood compact governs engagement. There is an obvious prevailing sentiment: "This is what we do here."

We love the *Pantsuit Politics* communities on Twitter and Instagram and rarely see the comment sections turn to dumpster fires. Why? The people participating in those spaces have context. They are almost all podcast listeners. Many have listened to our voices for hundreds of hours. They know who we are, what we're about, and why people might be following us. We don't have to explain that we don't attack one another, that insults are unwelcome, and that we don't reduce people to a single comment. People know. They show up with curiosity, compassion, and a respectful posture, even when they strongly disagree with us or other commenters.

Everything changes when one of our posts is shared widely. We can always feel the tipping point. Folks start rolling in who have no idea who we are, and many of them have decided based on the post they saw that they don't particularly care for us. The hate-posting gets real quickly. Some of our people, the people with the context, show up and gently try to guide the strangers like gracious hosts—*"Hi. You're new here, right? Let me show you how we do things."* At some point, everyone gets worn out with it, and we mercifully see the notifications start to dwindle.

You might be reading this thinking, *What a terrible attitude! Don't you want to get found?* Yes and no. We want to meet new people, certainly. Our work is enriched by a diversity of life experiences and perspectives. We also are keenly aware that we aren't for everyone. That's OK! This is, in fact, our thesis about the internet. It works best when we see it as a space for groups to gather instead of a wide-open public forum. Nothing on the internet is for everyone, and it's best for us to create spaces that cater to the people we're *for*.

Making the Connection

What are your favorite corners of the internet? Where is there enough context that you feel seen and heard surrounding the most important parts of who you are? Can you name the components of that context that you find valuable?

In *The Art of Gathering: How We Meet and Why It Matters*, author Priya Parker explains that every gathering of people benefits from placing some limits on who is in the room. She writes about a generous form of exclusion in which boundaries are created that enforce the purpose of the gathering: "If everyone is invited, no one is invited—in the sense of being truly held by the group. By closing the door, you create the room."[2] We find Parker's wisdom equally applicable in cyberspace.

If everyone is "here," no one can meaningfully interact.

So, yes, we want to meet new people on social media. But we want them to take the extra step of listening to our podcast.

That's how we keep our spaces meaningful for podcast listeners and readers. We ask people who show up to invest and buy into the context of the space. We welcome every single person who will do so, and we've seen beautiful things happen as a result.

Beth: In September 2020, my phone rang with the news I had dreaded. My parents had tested positive for COVID-19. This was my nightmare scenario. My mom's underlying health conditions make her particularly vulnerable to the virus, and I immediately felt like the earth was pulling me to its core to protect me from what might come next. Two days later, Mom was in an ambulance. For the next fifteen days, she would be hospitalized, all alone except for the nurses who cared for her with incredible kindness. My mom valued those nurses and their contact so much. They were her only link to the outside world, yet they were so covered in protective gear that she could not distinguish one from another.

I posted updates about my mom on Facebook and Instagram because . . . well, it was the only thing I could do to be helpful to my parents. I've never felt so powerless in my life, so I decided that I could at least be the family press secretary. I hoped that updating our friends and family on my mom's condition would take some pressure off my dad.

Nothing in my life experience could have prepared me for how our listeners would receive those updates. When I shared that Mom could receive cards and packages in the hospital, listeners from all over the country responded. My mom received artwork from children, poems from adults, books, puzzles, candles, neck massagers, socks, flowers, prayers, good wishes, and her favorites, long letters explaining why people listen to *Pantsuit Politics* and care about our family. She has kept every envelope, piece of construction paper, and gift tag. During our first postvaccination visit, I read all the cards. My heart has grown exponentially because of the tangible kindnesses my family received because of social media. I truly believe that Mom is alive today in huge part because of the support she received from so many people she's never met.

Find Your People and Purposes

Listeners and readers tell us about so many spaces in which context creates life-giving virtual connections. People connect over reading and writing books, cooking, faith practices and faith departures, TV shows they love, anime, care for specific pets and cars, painting and sculpting, selling a certain kind of shampoo. This is the real beauty of the internet's galaxy. We can all find our people if we look hard enough.

Sarah: When my youngest son, Felix, was six months old, we noticed that he was not really using his right hand. Six months old is too young to exhibit handedness, so that observation began a yearlong journey that ended with an MRI at Vanderbilt's Children's Hospital confirming what we had begun to assume after hours of internet research. Felix had a prenatal stroke and has hemiplegia on the right side of his body.

The first time I mentioned this on our podcast, a listener named Anna reached out to share that her son Max also has hemiplegia and that I should absolutely join the Children's Hemiplegia and Stroke Association and KISS Pediatric Stroke

Support Facebook groups. Anna said the groups had been a lifeline for her, and the support provided by fellow parents was invaluable. She was so right. These groups have helped us find shoes that can accommodate braces and therapies that help Felix expand his range of motion. Instead of tackling every problem on our own with our therapists, we have this amazing group of parents who are ready and willing to share the good and bad of having a child with a disability.

They also offer perspective. One of the hardest things about having a child with a disability is not letting that disability define everything about them. It's hard to know if a particular challenge is related to their issue or not. It's also hard to know what they're capable of—should you push them because they don't want to try or because it's actually hard for them? Instead of constantly being in my own head about all of this, I can simply go to Facebook and ask. Will Felix be able to ski? Yes! Are bedtime struggles related to the hemiplegia or him just being stubborn? A little of both! How much longer will it take him to learn to swim? With two siblings to push him, not long at all!

These pages have been a constant source of information and encouragement and perspective. I'm a better parent because of Felix, but I'm a better parent to Felix because of them.

....

So many listeners have echoed Sarah's experience. Finding people who are navigating a disease or condition can open up a world of information, connections to experts, and shared joy and hardships. These groups provide the shared context of a shared challenge. The unique difficulties of navigating the world with a disability or chronic disease can be incredibly isolating. The internet has connected those with that shared experience and provided the most life-giving of messages— you are not alone. Being connected (even with an internet-sized list of resources) to others with your same challenges doesn't automatically eliminate the struggle and hardship, but it certainly helps lessen it.

It's not only shared struggles that can provide valuable context inside social media. (In fact, we'd argue shared *grievance* is one of the most dangerous social media contexts.) When we surveyed listeners about where they feel most connected, a surprising number of people from all over the world mentioned Buy Nothing groups.

OF HOPE

The Buy Nothing Project, according to its website, is

> an international network of local gift economy Buy Nothing groups. Buy Nothing offers people a way to give and receive, share, lend, and express gratitude through a worldwide network of gift economies in which the true wealth is the web of connections formed between people who are real-life neighbors. We believe that communities are more resilient, sustainable, equitable, and joyful when they have functional gift economies.[3]

Buy Nothing groups create context through simple rules, including:

- Show your humanity
- Build trust
- Give freely

Buy Nothing groups exist all over the world—from Australia to Namibia to, yes, Paducah, Kentucky! The people in these groups don't all share one identity or struggle. They share a commitment to a certain set of principles. The values of the group provide the context. It's also clear that the people in the Buy Nothing groups don't interact *only* on social media within the Buy Nothing groups. However, sometimes it's enough to see the power and flourishing of online groups with context to recognize those *without context* and extricate yourself from them.

Keep the Political Context

Look, we're political podcasters. We both have more than sufficient experience with terrible political exchanges on social media. Sarah has wasted enough days being a keyboard ninja on Facebook to travel around the globe *at least* once, and Beth could fill a few books with the words she's expended trying to talk people off the ledge. It would seem as if politics provides context for these exchanges. After all, to some extent, we're all invested in politics. We're all connected through that shared relationship of residence, as we've spent many pages of this book establishing.

> The higher the stakes, the more important the context.

And yet, on social media, that context isn't quite enough. In part, the other important component of online interactions is how we define the stakes at hand. For example, the stakes in Sarah's conversations about Felix are as high as they get—love and devotion to her child. In theory, anyone with a child should be able to share that context, but people without the shared context of disability offer well-meaning but hurtful advice. The higher the stakes, the more important the context.

And the stakes (even if sometimes only perceived) within political conversations are high. If we're talking about abortion or capital punishment, we're talking about life and death. If we're talking about race and gender, we're talking about fundamental issues of identity that can also translate to life and death. If we're talking about taxes, we're talking about the literal money in someone's bank account. When stakes are high, emotions are high, and shared context is even more important.

Now that is not to say we should talk online only with those who agree with us because we share context. Sometimes shared context can open up space to see disagreement differently. If some random friend of a friend comments with an incendiary hot take on one of our political posts, then that opinion becomes the only context through which we can see them. We feel so strongly about the post (which is why we posted about it to begin with) that the stakes are high and the *only* context we have for them is their comment. Even with people we know well, if the stakes are high enough, our outside context for them shrinks.

We know it's tricky to ignore political posts. That's not always the right answer, but often "scroll on by and address this in person if it's someone you care about" is the best way to roll. We could write an entire book about better ways to interact around politics online. We suspect the simplest answer is the wisest: when it's really contentious, it probably doesn't belong online. True political debate, the kind that can enhance relationships or open hearts and minds, usually requires additional context.

This doesn't have to diminish our online experiences. Sometimes, whatever the context, the value in social media lies less in engagement and more in simple expression. Beth strongly prefers Twitter to Facebook. Sarah pressed her on why: "Is it because you think the exchanges are more valuable there?" And Beth answered honestly: "It's because the exchanges are less frequent and shorter." A tweet, whether it's about parenting, pop culture, or politics, can often just be. Maybe it's read, maybe not. Maybe someone responds, maybe they don't. Occasionally, we just have a thing to say and feel better for having said it. We don't need to run it to the ground with everyone from our mother to our husband's fifth-grade teacher chiming in with their two cents.

Making the Connection

Think back to your most heated political exchanges online. Do you talk to any of the people with whom you were commenting regularly in real life? Have you ever moved one of these discussions off-line and in person? What were the results?

We're not trying to increase the pressure on anyone participating in social media. As we said up front in this chapter, social media is operating on our brains in ways that we don't fully understand. What begins as a choice (to make a profile, to post a thing, to comment elsewhere, to join a group) is steadily influenced over time by powerful behavioral training from these technologies. It's also steadily influenced by extreme social pressures that are hard to recognize.

Social media is also fertile ground for sharing bad information. Again, we will leave the disinformation, misinformation, and conspiracy theories to the experts. Let's talk here about information that is true and incomplete. We post online—all of us, to some degree—because we're having an emotional reaction that we want to share. We're far enough into the social media galaxy that this is well understood, if not consciously articulated: if I want more followers (and I probably need more followers in order for my posts to be seen by anyone; we will curse the algorithms another day), I have to keep the emotional responses flowing.

The incentives created by the way our emotions motivate our like/click/share behavior (and the corresponding algorithmic rewards of like/click/share behavior) are . . . not great. It's why we tend to elevate some of the worst voices in politics ("Look at him, at it *again*! He's the worst!"). It's why we find ourselves anxious about truly bad state bills ("This is outrageous! This representative has got to go!") that are proposed in every session and never make it out of committee. It's why we share videos of awful events ("OMG, this is so sad! This should never happen!") before recognizing that people are retraumatized by videos that go viral.

It's so hard to talk about this because he is at it again and is truly the worst. The bill is probably outrageous, and the representative does need to go. The event was so sad and should never happen. We are not lying. We're having fair reactions. Our hearts are usually in the right place. And still, this behavior in the aggregate is doing merciless damage to all of us. We're staying simultaneously fired up and distracted and activated without a meaningful call to action.

Twitter. Ain't. Church.

Here's where we come to the Twitter portion of the chapter and why people need to stop acting like they're in the pews when they're just behind their keyboards. Social media presents us with a constant stream of stimuli along with a chorus of voices telling us what the singular appropriate response must be. Most of political Twitter is less about the story and more about how the story is told. The thing that happened gets lost. The tide of tweets sends the underlying facts and the people most impacted by those facts out to sea, and the shore is littered only with the classification of righteous and unacceptable takes. A story might materially change in the hours after it first lands online. No matter . . . the story isn't the story anymore. Our attention is captured by the people commenting on it and whether we are responding in the right way or the wrong way (and how ignorant or evil or hate-filled the wrong way-ers are), as ordained by the mob.

This phenomenon is unlikely to change because it has *some* value. The "takes" have taught many of us a great deal about perspectives we've previously not seen. Social media allows us to curate feeds filled with voices of people from communities and parts of the world that we don't know. We found a more accurate sensibility about the upcoming Brexit vote by following people in the UK than in reading American media about it. During the Arab Spring, social media provided invaluable perspective. When Texas endured extreme winter weather and power and water failures, social media helped us really understand the impacts.

For us, these observations have counseled in favor of curating our feeds based on current events instead of commentators. We're big fans of making lists relevant to events or just deciding "we're sticking with these three local reporters right now." We also no longer allow social media to tell us what to pay attention to. We subscribe to newsletters from reputable news organizations. Those emails, along with breaking news alerts from their websites, tell us what the driving stories of the day are.

When we're finding a story *only* on social media like "Truly Terrible Bill Filed by State Rep.," we approach it with skepticism. We usually run those stories against our own research because listeners and readers ask us questions about them, but we try to answer those questions and move on. We don't want our work to be driven by stories that are alarming but isolated and highly unlikely to materialize.

Establishing some guiding principles for ourselves online along with increasingly limiting our time on social media is helping us feel more grounded and clearheaded.

- We try to share content that we find personally enriching.
- We try to amplify diverse voices sharing good information.
- We pause before wading into trending topics.
- We think carefully about using hashtags in order to avoid opportunism or disrespect.

- We have a long-standing rule against sharing bad content. We don't repost anything for the purpose of telling people how bad/wrong/ignorant it is.
- We don't tweet-shame. If someone sends us a less-than-gracious comment, we don't share it as an invitation for people to defend us.
- We don't amplify attention-seeking posts that don't add value to our thoughts.

The important part for us is that online friendships are only a small part of a bigger ecosystem of connection that surrounds us. In our chapter on friendship, we pushed back on the idea that we have to be the same as our friends. If we lean too heavily on online friendships built upon a shared context, then we lose the chance to use our differences (and conflicts) to grow closer together.

We don't always get it right on social media; no one does! There are definitely days when we think we might be better off deleting our accounts. But for now, we aren't abstaining (except for Sarah, who picks one day each weekend to go completely off-line). We're doing our best to assess how social media can connect us to people and information in a healthy way. There's nothing easy or static about this exercise. Social media will continue to change. Until it is materially different, we're going to continue to do our best to navigate it with open hearts and critical eyes.

NOW What?

Where do you find the most context online? Where are you spending time without context? Do you see more benefits or burdens from the time spent in those spaces?

After you've considered these questions, consider this challenge: choose one social media account, group, or space to let go of. As you have your scrolling time (we see you doing that "revenge bedtime procrastination"), choose one space that's filled with context to give more of your attention.

10

Global Politics

Future Problem-Solving Forever

Beth: The first time Sarah invited me to a Korean Spa, I told her she had lost her whole entire mind. Her description of getting naked from head to toe upon entrance and staying that way while every millimeter of your bare self is exfoliated aggressively by another human being did not sound like my idea of a relaxing afternoon. But some part of me knew I'd end up there. Sarah Stewart Holland does not accept polite regrets.

On our next trip to Dallas, I dutifully accompanied her to King Spa & Sauna and ditched my clothes and dry skin. Despite being in and only in my body, it was a very out-of-body experience. It reminded me that I'm rarely in a place where the language and customs are unknown to me (and I'm never naked anywhere outside my own shower). I felt extraordinarily vulnerable and completely ordinary all at once. Here I was, both naked and anonymous. An outsider at home among bodies of all ages, shapes, colors, and sizes. Self-conscious about every flaw of my own body and completely unaware of the flaws in the bodies around me. Far from anything within my experience and relaxed, comfortable, restored.

We go back to King Spa & Sauna every time we're in Dallas. We don't know enough of South Korea to speak to its authenticity. But we do know that we have enormous respect and appreciation for the Korean people who care for us in such an impersonally personal way when we're there.

....

The great challenge of being a person living in the 2020s, as we see it, lies in reconciling the brain's in-group/out-group tendencies with the globe's gifts. Our brains take in an *enormous* amount of information, and the ability to categorize that information is literally essential to our survival. We are highly evolved to label friends and threats. And yet, Earth offers beauty and wisdom in every people, group, and terrain.

We can love and continue to build our distinct cultures while recognizing their limitations and appreciating all that other cultures have to offer. We can observe that our brains desire to sort all that bounty as good or bad and then encourage it to settle all the way down. We're Kentuckians, and we would be pleased to share our best biscuits, horse races, and bourbon with you. We also don't want to live in a world without paneer makhani, *The Great British Baking Show*, and Korean spas.

Throughout these pages, we've emphasized that we both need each other and that belonging to each other is difficult.

That's as true at the global level as it is within our families. We cannot thrive inside walls. The interconnectedness of living things on Earth is so rich and complex that we better understand the moon and Mars than Earth's deep oceans.[1] We do know that oceans contain 99 percent of living space on Earth. They regulate Earth's climate, produce 50 percent of the oxygen we breathe and absorb fifty times more carbon dioxide than the atmosphere, and provide us with food, medicine, transportation, and recreation.[2] We tend to think of five distinct oceans, but scientists are increasingly studying and accounting for marine connectivity, which is "the exchange of individuals, genetic sequences, or food and other material between regions or populations in the ocean."[3] Here's the point of this brief and nerdy aside on oceans (thank you for indulging Beth): Mother Nature simply does not recognize boundaries. We believe we should follow her lead.

Human life is no different and never has been. Our earliest ancestors migrated from Africa to Eurasia, then Australia, then the Americas.[4] We have pursued safety, resources, adventure, and riches. We have brought with us food, knowledge, mythology, customs, art, disease, and brutality. We are still doing so. If the COVID-19 pandemic revealed nothing else, it is how connected our fortunes are across the globe.

In America, discussions about global problems devolve into some version of a good guy/bad guy debate. Why should the US have to combat climate change when China creates so much pollution? Why should we fund programs abroad when there are people at home who have unmet needs? Isn't someone, somewhere, exaggerating the extent of fill-in-the-blank-obvious-problem?

Our thinking is stuck in the boundaries of modern maps, even as those maps have changed more than most Americans realize. For all of us who want to be better citizens of the globe, our working theory is that humanity is better understood by time than by location. We need to understand our past, deal as honestly as possible in our present, and look toward our future.

Making the Connection

Maps attest to how artificial and fluid boundaries are. Take a look at some old maps of your country. How long have the current boundaries been in place? How much change do you see happening over time? What factors do you think have informed that change?

Understanding the Past

Sarah: One of my greatest regrets in life is not taking more history classes in college. Deep down, college-age Sarah believed the problems facing our world were too urgent and unique to waste time learning about the problems of yesteryear. I can't tell you exactly when my perspective began to shift. I read Howard Zinn's *A People's History of the United States* and watched all eleven hours of Ken Burns's Civil War documentary. I also began to explore my own family's history. I gave Ancestry.com my credit card and spent hours and hours researching generations of Stewarts and Skidmores and Allens. I began the research desperate to discover my European ancestry but ended

up feeling more distinctly American after tracing eight generations in Kentucky alone.

Feeling connected to people who had lived through historical
events, like the American Revolution and the Great Depression,
helped me to see those moments as alive and relevant in a way
I hadn't before. The more I read and learned about our country's history, the more I saw relevance far beyond the fact that
someone I was related to had been there. The partisanship of
the post–Civil War press starts to seem similar to Breitbart and
OANN. The struggle for universal suffrage led by Frederick Doug-
lass and Susan B. Anthony and the way difficult conflicts over
identity and strategy split them apart can feel relevant to issues of
intersectionality present in our activism today. The robber barons
and rampant income inequality of the Gilded Age can leave even
the most skeptical among us thinking of Zuckerberg and Bezos
and Dorsey. And, of course, the pandemic of 1918 was just a
chapter in history until we were suddenly recording our own data
on infections, hospitalizations, and deaths due to a coronavirus.

Even in the face of existential threats, like climate change,
that seem like nothing the human race has faced before, I find
it oddly comforting to remind myself that simply isn't true. My
ancestors facing the bubonic plague certainly did not believe
thousands of tomorrows were assured to them or their off-
spring. Even my mother, as she was trained to duck and cover
as a young girl in the face of nuclear attacks, had to wonder if
the year 2022 would ever come into existence.

....

History doesn't assure us things will be OK, but it does
remind us that we are not only connected to those who

surround us now but also those who have come before us. Taking in one day of global news can quickly become overwhelming. China is dominating. Russia is meddling. Europe is dealing with tides of nationalism as the United Kingdom faces the fallout from Brexit. There are economic tragedies in Central America and ongoing conflicts between countries in Western Asia and Northern Africa. Every continent contains enough anxiety for each of its citizens several times over—much less for those watching from across the globe.

The story of change is never told in a single day, and we are never really alone.

But just like we talked about at the beginning of the book, anxiety shrinks our timelines. History gives us the chance to expand that timeline again and put anxiety in the back seat where it belongs. The best reported piece is always only part of the story because reporters are always limited in time and energy and resources. They've got to tell us what happened *now*. Historians take their time. Deadlines are few and far between when writing the annals of history. Looking back is an exercise in patience. One perspective simply won't suffice, and we see over time that moments of tremendous change are never created by a single person. That eases the pressure on all of us. Remembering the challenges of those who have come before—both similar and unique from those we face today—reminds us that the story of change is never told in a single day, and we are never really alone.

Dealing Honestly in the Present

Sarah is more oriented to the past and Beth to the future (more on that in a few pages). We hope in our work to combine those interests so that we can navigate the present as honestly as possible. It's impossible to do this perfectly. As we've discussed, our biases, experiences, and emotions impede our ability to see the dynamics in our families, friendships, and workplaces clearly. Shedding all that baggage on a global level is a big lift. We can't do it individually.

We *can* all contribute to the collective work of dealing honestly in the present. At the risk of sounding like a "The More You Know" commercial, learning matters. When we think about land area and population density, we're able to understand more accurately what we can offer one another in different parts of the world. When we learn more about a country's culture, we can better appreciate how present challenges arose and how they might be met. When we visit other countries (if those opportunities are available), we develop connections to people and places that change our perspectives on world events.

Sarah: Tunisia is a small Arab country of eleven million people in Northern Africa. Most Americans, if they've heard of it at all, associate the country with the 2011 Arab Spring when Tunisian street vendor Mohamed Bouazizi self-immolated and sparked wider prodemocracy protests across the region. That might be how I thought of Tunisia as well, had I not visited the country in 2008. My husband and I spent ten days riding camels, visiting Roman ruins, and eating more *brik a l'oeuf* than was reasonable.

We heard the call to prayer from the rooftops of the Medina and took a very long, very hot *louage* from the edge of the Sahara to the coast of the Mediterranean.

The people of Tunisia were kind and hospitable, but the language barrier was real. Most people in Tunisia speak Arabic or French, so there were no long cross-cultural conversations. And yet, my short time in Tunisia connected me forever to the people there. I can tell you where I was when I heard about the Arab Spring protests and how I felt when the Bardo Museum was attacked in 2015. I felt those moments as viscerally as I feel every mass shooting in America. I root for the people of Tunisia, currently the only democracy in North Africa, and encourage everyone who asks about my trip there to add this amazing country to their must-visit list. Tunisia became a part of me forever during those ten short days.

....

Travel is an amazing way to remind ourselves that as different as we are, our common humanity is always there for us to witness and embrace. However, crossing continents is impossible for many of us for reasons as diverse as humanity itself. Fortunately, travel is not the only way to see, hear, taste, or feel the globe. Memoirs, documentaries, music, art, and of course food, glorious food (Sarah highly recommends brik a l'oeuf) are some of the many ways we can expand our horizons. There is no place—no matter how small or how secluded—untouched by globalism's reach. That impact isn't always positive, but our interconnection is now a reality we no longer deny. Any opportunities that we have to amass a greater perspective on the world, we need to take. These experiences help reinforce two central points: (1) we are all connected and (2) as a result, we cannot be only one thing to one another.

In the US, politicians are frequently asked to identify which countries in the world pose the greatest threat to their country. It's not an absurd question. Geopolitical risks are real. As much as we wish for a world without weapons and war, we aren't there. The American public needs clear-eyed assessments that allow us to participate in holding leaders accountable for their foreign policy decisions.

The problem is that once we hear a country is a threat to the United States, it can be easy to think of them as a threat and nothing more, or to think about the threat as requiring one particular kind of response. It is always more complicated than that.

Making the Connection

What countries do you know about *only* through the lens of US opposition? Iran, North Korea, Rwanda—these are countries with complex histories and cultures that go far beyond their interactions with America. Take some time to explore countries that have become one-dimensional villains in our national narrative.

"The Longer Telegram" is a strategy paper about the US-China relationship. Authored anonymously and published by the Atlantic Council, it describes how America might intelligently counter the threat posed by "the rise of an increasingly authoritarian China under President and General Secretary Xi

Jinping." It advocates for a seven-part strategy. That strategy has domestic components: rebuilding America's economy, human capital, technology, and military power. It also involves defining the contours of our adversarial relationship with China, shoring up alliances throughout the world, and clearly determining the lines that China should be deterred from crossing. It emphasizes areas in which we should view China as a market competitor. *And* it discusses our need to collaborate with China around "mega-threats" of climate disruption, global pandemics, and nuclear security.[5]

The Biden administration echoed some of this philosophy. Secretary of State Antony J. Blinken has frequently said the US relationship with China will be "competitive where it should be, collaborative where it can be, adversarial where it must be."[6] This, we think, is a healthy, clear-eyed perspective. Reasonable people will disagree, sometimes vehemently, about what it means to put this philosophy into practice. As a framework for citizens, we find that it provides a crisp reminder that we aren't one thing to any other country, nor they to us.

Looking to the Future

Beth: Don't laugh. My favorite activity in middle and high school was Future Problem-Solving (that's FPS—IYKYK). I loved it so much that I now coach elementary and middle school teams. It's a six-step process tackled by a four-person team. It begins with a future scene that provides a little story about a particular place and time around a topic (like personalized medicine, oceans, wearable technology, etc.).

In the first step, the team examines the future scene and generates a list of potential challenges posed by the future scene. Teams use a list of sixteen categories—everything from business and commerce to arts and aesthetics to psychological health—to remind them to think broadly about the potential problems. In step two, teams select one challenge for focus. In writing this "underlying problem," they are not supposed to use an absolute verb. This requirement means that teams are supposed to think in terms of progress, not perfection. They don't "solve" the problem; they "improve," "reduce," "increase," etc. Then they use the same list of categories to generate potential solutions to the underlying problem, develop criteria to assess their solutions, and write an action plan for implementing their best solution.

It's impossible to overstate the impact that FPS has on my thinking. When I read about a potential treaty, I try to see it as an action plan and make sure that I can articulate the underlying problem it's trying to solve. This orientation reminds me that something like the Paris Accords is one approach of many possibilities. Government and politics is one of eighteen categories in the FPS process, which helps remind me that an underlying problem like climate change can and should be tackled from numerous angles. I'm getting better at remembering that the Joint Comprehensive Plan of Action or the Strategic Arms Reduction Treaty doesn't need to completely solve a problem to be effective. It just needs to improve desired outcomes or reduce negative ones. It just needs to make progress.

Several years into making the podcast together, Sarah and I realized not only had we both been on FPS teams in school but we had even competed against one another. I don't think that's an accident. I think you can see FPS in how we tackle issues together on the show. The steps we take today, for me, create new future scenes. Every action we take today will have consequences for future generations. I love the process of thinking about what challenges our kids might face based on the actions we're taking (and not taking) today.

....

The Millennium Project, a nonprofit global think tank connecting scholars, policy makers, futurists, and business planners, has identified fifteen future challenges—all of which transcend geographic borders.[7] Among those challenges are:

- How can everyone have sufficient clean water without conflict?
- How can population growth and resources be brought into balance?
- How can the global convergence of information and communications technologies work for everyone?
- How can the threat of new and reemerging diseases and immune microorganisms be reduced?

These challenges closely mirror the Seven Revolutions, which result from the Center for Strategic and International Studies' ongoing efforts to consider long-term global trends.[8] The Seven Revolutions are anticipated (and presently occurring) major changes to population, resources, technology, information, economics, security, and governance. Similar projects all over the world aim to identify the challenges ahead of us. It is fascinating reading. And sometimes it's scary.

We understand how overwhelming it is to consider global supply chains, the rapid spread of airborne pathogens, advancements in robotics, the ethics of editing our genes, and extreme water stress. We know our listeners and readers are worried about the future and that worry can be paralyzing. During a live show in Dallas, Texas (where we arrived fresh from King Spa), a ten-year-old girl stepped up to the microphone during our Q and A and told us she was fearful about the future. She asked us the question we hear from adults constantly (we even heard a prominent news anchor ask historian Doris Kearns Goodwin this question in a green room at MSNBC): Are we going to be OK?

We told that brave, precious girl the truth that we'll tell you: we don't know. It would be unwise and unfair to offer contrived assurances about our time on Earth together.

We do know that there is and will be very real suffering, hardship, oppression, and fear. And there's more.

We remain optimistic because we don't have to face any of that alone. The best part of FPS is that it takes place *on a team*. Orienting yourself to the future and its accompanying problems is significantly less overwhelming when you're with other people who are equally passionate about addressing them. What we saw in FPS is a dynamic we see in our real lives today. Hope grows when you hear another person voice an insight or bring clarity to something with which you were struggling. It is the ultimate reminder that the problem doesn't just live in your own head and you are not solely responsible for solving it. That's why we remain so optimistic because when we bring together talents, experiences, skills, and ideas across the world, we make so much more progress than if we were toiling alone.

And we *already* see the proof of that progress. We know that no one lives in averages, so it can be difficult to find comfort in data. Still, there are meaningful trends demonstrating that the world is improving even as you read these words. Child mortality is decreasing.[9] The number of people who live in poverty has fallen by over one hundred thousand *every day* for over twenty years. Wild polio has been eradicated from Africa.[10] In 2020, even when it felt like all public health news was tragic, the first mRNA vaccines were developed due in part to a global scientific effort.[11] Every year cities, countries, and corporations join the pledge to pursue net-zero emissions by the end of the century. In fact, all these groups combined have a carbon footprint greater than the emissions of the United States.[12]

── *Making the Connection* ─────

Where do you see optimism when you look across the globe? What gives you hope for the future?

────── OF **HOPE** ──────

One wildlife story makes Beth cry every time she thinks about it (and Beth is not the half of our duo most prone to tears): Beavers driven to extinction in the UK in the 1500s were successfully reintroduced in

Exmoor, England.[13] In a few weeks, the beavers built a small dam for the first time in four hundred years that created an instant wetland. Ben Eardley, a National Trust project manager, told BBC News, "We've already spotted kingfishers at the site, and over time, as the beavers extend their network of dams and pools, we should see increased opportunities for other wildlife, including amphibians, insects, bats and birds." If the beavers can make such a dramatic comeback and create so much possibility in the process, we can do it too.

Seemingly insurmountable obstacles are overcome by international research and collaboration every single day. The idea that "we are only one of billions" might leave us feeling powerless. We need to remove the word *only*. We are one of billions! We belong to a massive, growing human species. We cannot possibly comprehend all the suffering in our species. We also cannot possibly comprehend all the ingenuity in our species. We cannot make a difference on our own, and the good news is that we do not have to.

NOW What?

What other part of the world has influenced you? Do you have a strong family ancestry that was always a part of your family's story? Do you live near an immigrant community that has invited you in and shared their culture? Did you adopt a child from another part of the globe? Did you study abroad or take a vacation that forever changed how you saw a part of the world? How does being a global citizen show up in your life?

CONCLUSION

You just read a book about moving forward together when we're divided about basically everything. Now what?

We frequently hear from listeners and readers that caring about politics, civics, and their people is overwhelming. If you feel overwhelmed, you are not alone. Most of us wish to leave the world better than we found it. We want to leave you assured that you will, simply because of that desire. Our culture is focused on action items, and we know that you'd love to close this book with a bulleted to-do list. Certainly, there is work ahead, and we hope that something in these pages has inspired you about where you might want to focus your energy.

If you learned to see your parents' generational expectations more clearly, we hope you can see those generational expectations in that national political figure who drives you bananas. If you learned to see the government more clearly when you turn on your faucet, we hope you can share that perspective with your coworkers and show them we can share our whole and complete selves—including our curiosity—in the workplace. If you learned to tackle that tough political conversation with your child, we hope you take that strength into the next (inevitable) conflict at church. If you learned to leave your consumer mindset behind at your local school, we hope you also learned to stop just consuming globally but also to connect globally.

But beyond what we learn and what we do, it is significant that you exist simply with a heart for improving the world.

When you change your thoughts, you change the world. When you find a bit of softness around your dad's expectations, when you realize that your partner is searching for a sense of belonging with you, when you give a friend some space and ask a neighbor for a hand, you're establishing a new way of being that *will* have ripple effects. Seeing a coworker's coldness as an expression of fear, extending a little patience to the messy nonprofit, looking for governing instead of politics, finding the Suez Canal on a map when you hear about it in the news—every single expression of shared humanity matters. You are bringing grace to a world that needs it, and it will, in turn, bring that grace back to you.

Pema Chödrön, an American Tibetan Buddhist, describes the ancient practice of *tonglen*, which involves "taking and sending."

> Tonglen practice is a method of connecting with suffering— our own and that which is all around us, everywhere we go. It is a method for overcoming our fear of suffering and for dissolving the tightness of our hearts. Primarily it is a method for awakening the compassion that is inherent in all of us, no

matter how cruel or cold we might seem to be. We begin the practice by taking on the suffering of a person whom we know to be hurting and wish to help. For instance, if we know of a child who is being hurt, we breathe in with the wish to take away all of that child's pain and fear. Then, as we breathe out, we send happiness, joy, or whatever would relieve the child. This is the core of the practice: breathing in others' pain so they can be well and have more space to relax and open— breathing out, sending them relaxation or whatever we feel would bring them relief and happiness.[1]

This practice, which carries the familiarity of openhearted prayer to the two of us based on our religious traditions, is our go-to response when we grapple with news that seems unbearable. Even in a world without the unnecessary cruelty brought about by hatred and partisanship, there would be moments of unfathomable pain. We need practices that offer healing and resilience—which perhaps aren't that different from one another.

So, now what?

We will think some people are wrong for the rest of our lives, and some people will believe we couldn't be more off base in our beliefs. Sometimes the best response to these disagreements is to remain patiently in relationship with one another, offering the occasional challenge amid lots of space. Sometimes the best response is to wish the other person well and exit the relationship, recognizing that even when we choose not to be in contact, we remain connected.

We will never solve partisanship. We will never fix the fights. We will never prevent conflict. These truths are not the fault of media. They are not the fault of particular politicians. They are the human condition. As we hope you've seen throughout these pages, our political disagreement is a manifestation of our emotions, experiences, insecurities, passions, personalities, and interests. As long as we carry around the stuff of being human, we will part ways with one another's ideas, and we won't always be gracious about it.

The goal is not and has never been to have one grace-filled conversation, dust off our hands, and say "Fixed it!" We strengthen connection not by agreeing or resolving tension. We strengthen connection by recognizing that our unique identities are what bring us together. We honor the specialness of each human being—be it our parent or our president—by letting it exist and not demanding conformity. We honor the divine in others and in ourselves. This does not mean condoning differences that are harmful in pursuit of agreement. It just means acknowledging that agreement cannot be the goal in a planet as big and diverse as ours. It can't even be the goal inside a partnership between two people. Connection is the goal because connection is the reality—even in the face of the most challenging political controversies of our age. And conversation—not to solve conflict but to recognize that connection—can get us closer.

When we see conflict as a problem to be solved, we see our connection to one another through the lens of negativity and lack. And yet, conflict is only a manifestation of our connection, and our relationships to one another are not something to be managed or controlled or fixed. Our connection to one another is why we are here. There are so many things we do during our time on this planet—we toil and rest, we create and tear down, we grow and decay—but there is very little we do that we do alone. We are ever-present in one another's lives—from those who hold us close to those who live on the other side of the globe. We are both incredibly unique as individuals and incredibly connected through our ubiquity. No one else can bring what you can bring to this moment in time, and that is also true of every other human on planet Earth.

Politics is about power and the exchange of that power. It functions in a zero-sum environment most of the time, but to apply that framework widely is what is harming so many of our relationships. Life is about presence. Connection is not zero-sum. What we hope we've shown you throughout this book is that our *presence* in one another's lives has to become more visible than our conflicts. In our families, that presence can be a daily text or shared vacation. In our friendships, that presence can be a mutual devotion to the home team or reaching out for help in a moment of need. In our communities, that presence can be a hard conversation at a board meeting or a prayer of gratitude every time you flush a toilet. In our nation and world, that connection can be a shared moment of pain or a shared ancestry stretching back generations.

These shared constellations of connection give us an opportunity to look up and see the same stars pointing up toward a common destination—even when the clouds of conflict darken our path. We have the chance to search the dark corners of our own hearts for where we are obstacles in the journey, to search together in the night for the light of those shared stars, and even to decide we would like to continue a part of the journey alone. Whatever we decide, the courage to examine these most fundamental of connections with curiosity will inevitably transform us and our world.

Now what? Keep moving forward. Keep showing up with all of your gifts and your desires and your discernment about how you can contribute more by loving more, even when you disagree with your people about basically everything for always.

When Connections Are Too Toxic and Need to Be Severed

Sometimes political disagreements move out of the realm of opinion and into manipulation. Whether it is our parents or partners, our kids or best friends, we need to take care that we are not trying to control one another. When it feels like one person is trying to deprive the other of agency, it's time to make a change. Control can take a lot of forms. When we hear stories from people who are being shamed over political views (especially when that shame is cast in religious terms), it sets off alarm bells for us. We cannot sustainably stay in relationships if one person is trying to exercise power over the other.

We also want to recognize that political disagreements are not hypothetical. There are times when our fundamental dignity is devalued by another person's political perspective.

No one should be degraded in any relationship—familial, romantic, or otherwise—especially not in relationships that should provide them with the most trust, love, and support.

For many of us, our political participation connects to a sense of calling. It's tempting to minimize our disagreements, as though anything political is an ultimately trivial concern. While we believe it's important to keep politics in its place (meaning, it cannot occupy all of the space in life, work, or relationships), we also know that politics matters. Many of us feel called on a deep level to work toward greater justice in the world. We have to be in relationships that support our callings. If someone in our life is at odds with the work we believe we are here on the earth to do, that relationship is likely to break down.

These are hard admissions for us. We have built our work around the idea that good, thoughtful conversation can bring us closer together. We wholeheartedly know it to be so. We also know that not every gap within every relationship can or should be bridged. It is important to say so.

If you are in a situation that is not safe for your body, mind, spirit, children, money, or heart, we want you to know that you are not alone. We want you to know how many people are waiting to wrap their arms around you on the other side of this difficult moment. And we want to gently encourage you to reach out today, whether it's to a member of your community or to an expert. We know that taking that step to reach out is not easy. We also know that it is worth it. You deserve to be loved wholeheartedly and to be treated with kindness and dignity and respect.

We can't know everyone's situation. But we do know that these organizations and many like them are waiting to serve you.

National Domestic Violence Hotline 1-800-799-SAFE (7233)

National Child Abuse Hotline 1-800-4-A-CHILD (422-4453)

Family Violence Prevention Center 1-800-313-1310

Families Anonymous 1-800-736-9805

Gay and Lesbian National Hotline 1-888-843-4564

Youth Crisis Hotline 1-800-448-4663

National Suicide Prevention Lifeline 1-800-273-8255

The Trevor Project Hotline 1-866-488-7386

These resources are all based in the United States. If you are reading this book outside of the United States, suicide.org will allow you to connect with hotlines in your country. Domestic shelters.org lists international resources to support domestic violence survivors.

ACKNOWLEDGMENTS

We signed the contract for this book in December of 2020. With a vaccine imminent, we thought we'd be writing our manuscript post-pandemic. To say our optimism was misplaced is a laughable understatement. For several months, we attempted to write this book at home surrounded by children who were attempting to virtually learn. We were emptied out physically, emotionally, and spiritually.

Eventually, we escaped for a weekend away and hammered out the first draft of the book you now hold. In retrospect, being pushed to our limits was the perfect place to write about how to connect in the face of conflict when taking a single step forward is the last thing you want to do. We owe an unending amount of gratitude to all the people in our lives who supported us as we took those first shaky steps and the long journey that came after.

To our husbands, Nicholas and Chad, thank you for supporting us. Our work is demanding and unpredictable, and your support requires strength and flexibility. Thank you. To our beloved children, you motivate us, teach us, frustrate us, and inspire us. Every word we write is with you in mind.

To our parents, all we ever want is to make you proud. To our friends, fellow church members, board colleagues, and neighbors who make up the crucial layers of support and belonging we describe in this book, thank you for doing life with us.

To our agent, Sharon, thank you for valuing our words and believing they deserve to be published. To Kelsey and the team at Revell, you have been a dream to work with and have healed old publishing wounds we didn't even know we had.

To our *Pantsuit Politics* team, thank you for riding with us through the wild, wild west of an industry that's only constant is change. To our listeners, thank you for giving us lives we couldn't have dreamed up for ourselves.

NOTES

Introduction

1. Sarah Stewart Holland and Beth Silvers, *I Think You're Wrong (But I'm Listening): A Guide to Grace-Filled Political Conversations* (Nashville: Thomas Nelson, 2019), 21.

Chapter 1 Our Families of Origin

1. See, for example, David N. Daniels, "Nature AND Nurture: Acquiring an Enneagram Type," https://drdaviddaniels.com/articles/nature-and-nurture/.

2. Alyson Schafer, "5 Ways Siblings Shape Kids More Than Their Parents Do," HuffPost Canada, May 29, 2017, https://www.huffingtonpost.ca/2017/05 /29/how-siblings-shape-you_n_16869940.html.

3. Recorded Zoom interview with Sarah, January 26, 2020.

4. Viviana A. Zelizer in Jennifer Senior, *All Joy and No Fun: The Paradox of Modern Parenthood* (New York: Ecco, 2014), 10.

5. Giulia M. Dotti Sani and Judith Treas, "Educational Gradients in Parents' Child-Care Time across Countries, 1965–2012," *Journal of Marriage and Family*, April 19, 2016, http://doi.org/10.1111/jomf.12305.

6. "Mitch McConnell, SOTU, and How to Be a White Ally (with Dr. David Campt)," *Pantsuit Politics* (podcast), February 8, 2019, https://www.pantsuit politicsshow.com/show-archives/2019/2/7/how-to-be-a-white-ally-with-dr -david-campt.

Chapter 2 The Families We Create

1. Eli J. Finkel, Chin Ming Hui, Kathleen L. Carswell, and Grace M. Larson, *The Suffocation of Marriage: Climbing Mount Maslow without Enough Oxygen,*

Northwestern University and University of Chicago, October 31, 2013, https://faculty.wcas.northwestern.edu/eli-finkel/documents/InPress_FinkelHuiCarswellLarson_PsychInquiry.pdf.

2. Maija Kappler, "Survive This COVID-19 Winter by Avoiding Conflict with Your Roommates," HuffPost, November 9, 2020, https://www.huffingtonpost.ca/entry/covid-winter-roommates_ca_5f99da50c5b6aab57a0eff72.

3. Emma Ailes, "'Covid Ended Our Marriage': The Couples Who Split in the Pandemic," BBC World Service, December 3, 2020, https://www.bbc.com/news/world-55146909.

4. Matt Dooley, "I Know a Marriage Killed by QAnon and Trump, with Help from Alienation," *The Guardian*, October 21, 2020, https://www.theguardian.com/commentisfree/2020/oct/22/i-know-a-marriage-killed-by-qanon-and-trump-with-help-from-alienation.

Chapter 3 Raising Citizens

1. The exact origin of this quote cannot be determined, but it is frequently attributed to Ellen Cantarow.

2. American Psychological Association, "Stress in America™ 2020," October 2020, https://www.apa.org/news/press/releases/stress/2020/sia-mental-health-crisis.pdf.

Chapter 4 Friendships

1. W. W. Hartup, "Social Relationships and Their Developmental Significance," *American Psychologist* 44, no. 2 (1989): 120–26.

2. Daniel A. Cox, "The State of American Friendship: Change, Challenges, and Loss," Survey Center on American Life, June 8, 2021, https://www.americansurveycenter.org/research/the-state-of-american-friendship-change-challenges-and-loss/.

3. Julianne Holt-Lunstad et al., "Loneliness and Social Isolation as Risk Factors for Mortality: A Meta-Analytic Review," *Perspectives on Psychological Science* 10, no. 2 (March 11, 2015): 227–37, https://doi.org/10.1177/1745691614568352.

Chapter 5 Workplaces

1. Heather R. Huhman, "The Hidden Benefits of Happy Co-Workers (Infographic)," *Entrepreneur*, October 8, 2014, https://www.entrepreneur.com/article/238122.

2. "New Survey Reveals 75% of Millennials Expect Employers to Take a Stand on Social Issues," Glassdoor, September 25, 2017, https://www.glassdoor.com/blog/corporate-social-responsibility/.

Chapter 6 Community—Churches and Nonprofits and Schools

1. Lee Ann Womack, "I Hope You Dance," *I Hope You Dance*, 2000, produced by Mark Wright and Frank Liddell.

2. Jeffrey M. Jones, "U.S. Church Membership Down Sharply in Past Two Decades," Gallup, April 18, 2019, https://news.gallup.com/poll/248837/church-membership-down-sharply-past-two-decades.aspx.

3. Sam Carr, "How Many Ads Do We See in a Day in 2021?" PPC Protect, February 15, 2021, https://ppcprotect.com/how-many-ads-do-we-see-a-day/.

4. Patti Digh, "A Strong Offer," https://www.pattidigh.com/strong-offer/.

Chapter 7 Local and State Government

1. Al Tompkins, "How Rush Limbaugh's Rise after the Gutting of the Fairness Doctrine Led to Today's Highly Partisan Media," Poynter, February 17, 2021, https://www.poynter.org/reporting-editing/2021/how-rush-limbaughs-rise-after-the-gutting-of-the-fairness-doctrine-led-to-todays-highly-partisan-media/.

2. Damon Centola, "Why Social Media Makes Us More Polarized and How to Fix It," *Scientific American*, October 15, 2020, https://www.scientificamerican.com/article/why-social-media-makes-us-more-polarized-and-how-to-fix-it/.

3. Clara Hendrickson, "Local Journalism in Crisis: Why America Must Revive Its Local Newsrooms," The Brookings Institution, November 12, 2019, https://www.brookings.edu/research/local-journalism-in-crisis-why-america-must-revive-its-local-newsrooms/.

Chapter 8 National Politics

1. "Transcript: Ezra Klein Interviews Nadine Burke Harris," *New York Times*, March 9, 2021, https://www.nytimes.com/2021/03/09/podcasts/ezra-klein-podcast-nadine-burke-harris-transcript.html.

2. "Adverse Childhood Experiences (ACEs)," CDC, accessed July 27, 2021, https://www.cdc.gov/violenceprevention/aces.

3. James Truslow Adams, *The Epic of America* (Garden City, NY: Blue Ribbon Books, 1941), 404.

4. "The 1619 Project," *New York Times*, August 14, 2019, https://www.nytimes.com/interactive/2019/08/14/magazine/1619-america-slavery.html.

5. Judith Shklar, *The Faces of Injustice* (New Haven: Yale University Press, 1990), 151.

Chapter 9 Social Media

1. Shoshana Zuboff, "The Coup We Are Not Talking About," *New York Times*, January 29, 2021, https://www.nytimes.com/2021/01/29/opinion/sunday/facebook-surveillance-society-technology.html.

2. Priya Parker, *The Art of Gathering: How We Meet and Why It Matters* (New York: Riverhead Books, 2018), 38.

3. "The Fine Print," The Buy Nothing Project, accessed July 27, 2021, https://buynothingproject.org/the-fine-print-2/#Join.

Chapter 10 Global Politics

1. Dan Stillman, "Oceans: The Great Unknown," NASA, October 8, 2009, https://www.nasa.gov/audience/forstudents/5-8/features/oceans-the-great-unknown-58.html.

2. "Why Should We Care about the Ocean?" (infographic), National Ocean Service, last updated February 26, 2021, https://oceanservice.noaa.gov/facts/why-care-about-ocean.html.

3. Catherine Offord, "How Interconnected Is Life in the Ocean?," The Scientist, November 1, 2019, https://www.the-scientist.com/magazine-issue/how-interconnected-is-life-in-the-ocean--66615.

4. Erin Blakemore, "Human Migration Sparked by Wars, Disasters, and Now Climate," *National Geographic*, February 28, 2019, https://www.nationalgeographic.com/culture/article/migration.

5. "The Longer Telegram toward a New American China Strategy," Atlantic Council, accessed July 27, 2021, https://www.atlanticcouncil.org/content-series/atlantic-council-strategy-paper-series/the-longer-telegram/.

6. Antony J. Blinken, "Secretary Antony J. Blinken, National Security Advisor Jake Sullivan, Director Yang and State Councilor Wang at the Top of Their Meeting," US Department of State, March 18, 2021, https://www.state.gov/secretary-antony-j-blinken-national-security-advisor-jake-sullivan-chinese-director-of-the-office-of-the-central-commission-for-foreign-affairs-yang-jiechi-and-chinese-state-councilor-wang-yi-at-th/.

7. The Millennium Project, accessed July 27, 2021, http://www.millennium-project.org/projects/challenges/.

8. Center for Strategic and International Studies, "Seven Revolutions" (factsheet), https://csis-website-prod.s3.amazonaws.com/s3fs-public/171114_Seven-Revolutions-Brochure-2017.pdf.

9. Julius Probst, "Seven Reasons Why the World Is Improving," BBC Future, January 10, 2019, https://www.bbc.com/future/article/20190111-seven-reasons-why-the-world-is-improving.

10. Chris Weller, "A Top Economist Just Put the Fight against Poverty in Stunning Perspective," *Business Insider*, October 17, 2017, https://www.businessinsider.com/max-roser-puts-fight-against-poverty-in-stunning-perspective-2017-10.

11. Rob Picheta, "2020 Was a Terrible Year. But the World's in Better Shape Than You Might Think," CNN, December 25, 2020, https://www.cnn.com/2020/12/25/europe/2020-improving-world-recap-scli-intl/index.html.

12. "Commitments to Net Zero Double in Less Than a Year" (press release), United Nations Framework Convention on Climate Change, September 21, 2021, https://unfccc.int/news/commitments-to-net-zero-double-in-less-than-a-year.

13. "Beavers Build First Exmoor Dam in 400 Years," BBC News, November 30, 2020, https://www.bbc.com/news/uk-england-somerset-55125932.

Conclusion

1. This has been adapted from Pema Chödrön, "Tonglen: Bad In, Good Out," Lion's Roar, October 2, 2017, https://www.lionsroar.com/tonglen-bad-in-good-out-september-2010/.

Sarah Stewart Holland and Beth Silvers cohost the popular podcast *Pantsuit Politics* and coauthored *I Think You're Wrong (But I'm Listening): A Guide to Grace-Filled Political Conversation* (2019). *Pantsuit Politics* has been featured in the *New York Times*, *The Atlantic*, *The Guardian*, MSNBC's *Morning Joe*, as well as *Parents* and *Elle* magazines.

Both Sarah and Beth attended Transylvania University in Lexington, Kentucky, and then received their Juris Doctors (Sarah from American University and Beth from the University of Kentucky). Sarah began her career as a congressional staffer, campaign aide, and blogger and social media consultant. She lives in Paducah, Kentucky, where she served a term as a city commissioner and sits on the board of numerous civic organizations.

Beth has practiced law and served as a human resources executive and business coach. Beth lives in Union, Kentucky, and serves on several local boards of directors. Sarah and Beth speak frequently to universities, businesses, and civic organizations about improving political dialogue. Sarah shares life with her spouse, Nicholas, and children Griffin, Amos, and Felix; Beth with her spouse, Chad, and children Jane and Ellen. Sarah's dog, Cookie, and Beth's dog, Lucy, are beloved and frequent contributors to their work.

Stay connected with
Sarah and Beth

 **@pantsuitpolitics**